THE PRODUCT

Novel Writing PREP

A 30-DAY PLANNER THAT PREPARES YOU TO WRITE 50,000 WORDS IN ONE MONTH

USA TODAY BESTSELLING AUTHOR
MONICA LEONELLE

Copyright © 2020 by Monica Leonelle.
All rights reserved.

This material is provided "as-is" without any warranty of any kind. Every effort has been made to ensure the accuracy of this book; however, errors and omissions may occur. The publisher assumes no responsibility for any damages arising from the use of this book.

No portion of this book may be reproduced or transmitted—electronically, mechanically, graphically, or by any other means, including photocopying, recording, taping, or by any information storage or retrieval system—without written permission from the publisher.

Address inquiries to team@theworldneedsyourbook.com

Visit our website: **TheWorldNeedsYourBook.com**

Library of Congress Cataloging-in-Publication Data

Leonelle, Monica.
Novel writing prep.

ISBN 978-1-63566-007-4 (pbk.)

Manufactured in the United States of America

First Edition
First Printing
Author: Monica Leonelle
Cover Design: Monica Leonelle

TABLE OF CONTENTS

Introduction 1

Why I Wrote Novel Writing Prep 7

Day 1: Idea to Concept 25

Day 2: Theme 33

Day 3: Worldviews 39

Day 4: Groups 45

Day 5: Characters 52

Day 6: Character Relationships 58

Day 7: Character Fatal Flaws 63

Day 8: Character False Beliefs 72

Day 9: Character Motivations and the Fatal Flaw 79

Day 10: Character Goals and the False Beliefs 86

Day 11: A Quick and Dirty Plot 98

Day 12: The Setup 108

Day 13: Characters in the Orphan Energy 117

Day 14: The Response 122

Day 15: Characters in the Wanderer Energy 132

Day 16: The Attack 137

Day 17: Characters in the Warrior Energy 145

Day 18: The Resolution 149

Day 19: Characters in the Martyr Energy 156

Day 20: Thematic Elements: Group and Character Symbolism 160

Day 21: Thematic Elements: Theme, Setting, and Worldbuilding 167

Day 22: Setting and World: Place 173

Day 23: Setting and World: Life and Culture 176

Day 24: Setting and World: History, Technology, and Law 179

Day 25: The Treatment 182

Day 26: Outlining 0-25% 186

Day 27: Outlining 25-50% 192

Day 28: Outlining 50-75% 198

Day 29: Outlining 75-100% 203

Day 30: Fill in the Gaps 210

Next Steps 212

Acknowledgements

About the Author

*To Onemind,
where this book started.*

INTRODUCTION

WELCOME TO 30 DAYS OF NOVEL PREP!

I'm going to get right to it—you want to write a novel. And you would ideally like to make that first draft happen fast.

- Maybe you are trying to increase your speed at publishing, or maybe you are on a tight deadline with your publisher.

- Maybe you are an aspiring author who wants to participate in National Novel Writing Month (#NaNoWriMo) for the first (or twelfth) time.

- Maybe you don't have a deadline or a plan, but just want to improve your writing craft in 30 days.

All are welcome!

30 DAYS TO A BETTER NOVEL

For the next 30 days, I'll be sharing the most important 30 snippeted lessons from my Story Symmetry Framework.

Each lesson includes a short description of the concept or exercise we are learning for the day, several examples from popular franchises (usually modern books that have been turned into movies or television shows), and prompts (questions) that help you apply the concept to your novel. I also have a section on challenges and gotchas called "Feeling Stuck?" in case you, well, feel stuck at any point.

HOW TO USE THIS BOOK

Do I really have to do it over 30 days?

The lessons are designed to take about 20-30 minutes each, so you could probably get through the entire book over a long weekend or even a focused several hours a night after work for a week.

Additionally, once you've read the book and understand the concepts behind the prompts, you can get the companion workbook called *Novel Writing Prep Companion Workbook (The Productive Novelist Workbooks #1)* and work through that for each new novel you are plotting.

If you really love my style of outlining, you may

INTRODUCTION

also want to check out *Story Symmetry for Novelists: Tune Your Story Into Harmony and Alignment to Create a Better Reading Experience (The Productive Novelist #5)*.

Both of these supplementary resources are available at all online retailers.

Can I use this book as a pantser (someone who writes by the seat of their pants)?

I am agnostic regarding the age-long debate over pantsing vs. plotting; in my opinion, it doesn't matter in the slightest what phase of your writing you discover your story. All that matters is that your best story makes it into print.

You can discover parts of your story at all points in your writing—outlining, drafting, and editing.

If you are a plotter, this is a great book for preparing a detailed outline of your novel before you write.

If you are a pantser, you can use this book to edit your draft into submission after you write.

While this book was designed to be used before writing the first draft, writing craft does not change just because you have more words in front of you!

Do I have to do all the lessons?

No, you don't. Feel free to skip any lessons that you don't want to do. If you do even one lesson you will set yourself up for greater success with your novel, because you've made more informed decisions about your story before writing it.

Additionally, you can just read along with the book to learn more about storytelling and writing craft. We internalize story naturally, so just reading the book will likely improve your ability to write your next novel!

Will I encounter spoilers in this book?

Yes. I use lots of examples from modern stories to illustrate specific storytelling concepts. You may encounter spoilers for any story across books, movies, television, plays, and other storytelling mediums if it was released before the publication date of this book.

That said, the examples I pull are primarily from these franchises (including the books and movies):

- The *Harry Potter* series by J.K. Rowling
- *The Fault in Our Stars* by John Green
- *The Hunger Games* trilogy by Suzanne Collins
- *The Twilight Saga* by Stephenie Meyer
- *A Song of Ice and Fire* series by George R.R. Martin
- *The Martian* by Andy Weir

You do not need to have consumed any of these books or movies to understand the concepts in this book, but it may help!

INTRODUCTION

Is this really going to help me through National Novel Writing Month?

(Or an equally challenging sprint to write 50,000 fiction words in one month?)

Yes, you can write 50,000 good words on your novel in as little as a month, as long as you prepare yourself.

After helping thousands of authors develop the skills to hit huge word counts in a short period of time, I've found one thing in common across all authors, at all skill levels, from those who have never written a novel to those who publish professionally.

This one thing not only helps writers get their book to make sense (and read well!) on paper, but also helps them write it faster in the first place.

And it's simple: You must know what you are going to write before you write it.

Most writers can at least double their writing speed (some can triple it), meaning they can do twice as many words in the same time period as they were doing before.

Additionally, these writers encounter fewer bouts of writer's block and are more likely to see their book in print down the line.

It worked for me (and continues to work for me) and I believe that it can work for you too.

If you want to learn more about writing faster, you'll probably like my books *The 8-Minute Writing Habit*, *Write Better, Faster,* and *Dictate Your Book.* They are books 2, 3, and 4 of *The Productive Novelist* series, respectively.

WHO ARE YOU?

My name is Monica Leonelle and I have been publishing fiction since 2011. I write young adult fantasy, science fiction, and romance under Solo Storm and another pen name. Between these two pen names I have about 20 books. My urban fantasy novella *The Last Daughter* hit the *USA Today* bestseller list in 2017 as part of a boxed set.

I've also written over 10 nonfiction books about writing, editing, publishing, marketing, and business. You can learn more about my work at:

» **theworldneedsyourbook.com**

That's not much of an introduction, I know—but I also know that many of you are here for prepping your novel, not hearing my life story. I've shared my story around struggling through my first few novels and novellas in the next section, but I have no qualms if you skip that and go straight into the 30 days. However, if you're curious, you'll learn some juicy and dramatic details about how I got started as an author.

WHY I WROTE NOVEL WRITING PREP

Like many of you, I've been a reader for years, with a special place in my heart for young adult books as well as fantasy. My favorite book series as a child was the *Chronicles of Narnia*, and I had refound my love of reading and writing during my teenage years through the *Harry Potter* and *Twilight Saga* series. I had recently finished the last of *The Mortal Instruments* series and all I wanted was to get lost in some more amazing young adult fantasy that made me feel something.

At the time, I was in my early twenties, married, and in a relationship that had fallen apart before the wedding. I had married him in part because of my incessant people pleasing tendencies. I was the "good girl" who honored my commitments, plus the wedding invitations had already been sent and I didn't want to disappoint people or "fail."

Novel Writing Prep

Looking back, I now understand why I loved fiction so much during this time in my life—I desperately needed a place to escape from my challenging reality. But the thing that shifted me from reading books to writing them was that I had run out of content that excited me. I had loved being a part of so many fandoms for so many years... but where was the next big one that could capture my attention and keep me up until all hours of the night?

Because of my failing marriage, I took a job in Atlanta, a solid 12-hour drive from Chicago where my husband lived. Of course, my pattern of finding abusive men came right along with me in my new boss, who broke a chair in a fit of fury during my first week on the job. It was not a pleasant work environment, but I made a friend at work, whom I'll call T. I started sending T little bits of the young adult urban fantasy about angels that had been brewing in my head. She would send me emails back: "Love it! More please." My new book was moving forward! I was so excited to have one fan who I could try to write to.

FICTION OR CORPORATE?

It wasn't until about a year later that I left the job and got serious about writing my book. At around the same time, fiction authors like Amanda Hocking and John Locke were uploading their novels to a new Amazon program called Kindle Direct Publishing—

and making boatloads of money to quit their jobs. I had always wanted to work for myself after never really finding my place in corporate. I knew I wanted to have a bestselling fiction book and series, but I had no idea how to do it.

I had self-published one book already—a nonfiction book about social media in 2009, when Twitter was really taking off with corporations. It flopped in terms of sales, but I secured not one but two high-paying jobs with it, so technically I did make my money back.

Still, I felt anxious about repeating my many mistakes with that book with my fiction. But I also knew that I couldn't keep working in corporate, as my personality, no matter how I tried, didn't seem suited for the jobs I was doing.

My biggest self-sabotage was that I had too many big ideas, many of which weren't practical to implement, and many of which were a hard sell in a workplace. I was far too creative and wild to fit in, and this clashed with the workplace goal of playing it safer. I also struggled with getting my mind to focus on the task at hand, as whenever I had a new idea, my mind and all my energy would build momentum for that idea, even if I was supposed to be working on something else. I've since learned that I can succeed at channeling my energy into my own projects, but I struggle to maintain energy long-term for others' ideas and goals.

I knew that I needed to permanently quit the workforce so I could thrive instead of merely survive, but I wasn't exactly a trust fund baby! I also needed a paycheck.

As I finished my book, I had to decide: Did I want to go all in on marketing the book, which I knew would take my attention and energy away from my new job (and possibly get me fired or labelled a poor performer in the workplace)? Or did I want to set the book aside, likely for years, and do everything I could to make my new job at a growing start-up work? I didn't have enough energy and time to do both. Was I going for the creative life or the secure paycheck?

I decided to do the book, because I couldn't fathom putting it on hold. I still went to work, but I certainly wasn't putting in start-up level hours. I was gliding by and saving all of my energy for the after hours, when I would write and market my book.

THE LAUNCH

My book launched, I sold a few hundred copies, and hooray—many people loved the story and were waiting for the second book!

I also got a bunch of feedback in my book reviews that pointed to inability to tell a story—which was ultimately incredibly helpful. People liked the story but many felt it was wandering quite a bit. I later figured out that I wasn't giving the story a proper story structure, which was causing issues with the emotional resonance of the book.

I set my second book launch date for July of that same year and then... my husband and I separated. It happened very quickly, when he started talking about children and I realized, "I don't want to bring children into this relationship." I wasn't able to leave the relationship for myself, but when I thought of putting my children through all of the fights, name-calling, object-throwing, screaming and yelling, and violent outbursts, it was a clear hell no for me.

In the aftermath of my separation, I found myself under-eating and abusing alcohol to numb the pain and exhaustion of divorce. A few months later, my pattern of filling myself with alcohol instead of food had me falling headfirst into a glass table at a co-worker's apartment. Just weeks after that, the company I was working for was bought by Paypal and my lackluster performance had me out the door. Left with no energy to write the second book in the series and no steady paycheck, I knew I needed to make some changes in my life.

A HAPPY COMPROMISE

I decided not to get another full-time job, despite having offers. I felt I knew where that road led—me ultimately unfulfilled and wasting the company's time and resources, and they eventually having to let me go or relinquish me to a dark corner of their company where I would work on low-impact projects. I wanted to write, but I had a lot to learn about fiction, and I wasn't exactly in the right state of mind to start churning out novels as a profession. So instead, I chose a middle of the road path of freelance and consulting for companies while also learning everything I could about writing fiction. This assuaged my guilt of not being truly present for the company I was working with, while giving me time to pursue my real dreams.

I knew the next step in my writing career. As much as I valued my creativity and expression, I needed to write a marketable story. I needed to embrace story structure and increase my understanding of it. So I went to Amazon and purchased 60 print books on story structure. I stacked them against the wall next to my TV, so I couldn't forget to study, study, study. I read one of these books every day for several months, in between the emotional darkness and tears of my life as I knew it crumbling around me.

HOW STORY STRUCTURE CHANGED MY LIFE

As I read, something changed in me. I felt like I was unlocking the secret to success at fiction and storytelling. I had been so resistant to story structure before, wanting to do it my way and be unique. Perhaps you resonate with some of these?

- I wanted to write for fun and outlining felt like work
- I didn't think I could be imaginative or inspired if I outlined first
- I wanted to be the artist, not the business person
- I didn't think story structure was a part of my writing process
- I worried that outlining would make the story feel boring while writing it
- I didn't want to outline in a logical or linear structure as it felt like the opposite of creativity
- I worried about the time that outlining took and wondered if I was better served writing words
- I felt justified in not outlining because [insert successful author here] doesn't outline or *never* outlined and did just fine

But as I read those books and I started to implement the story structure advice within them, I learned how wrong I was about every single one of these. My beliefs were false, and I needed a new set of beliefs to move forward on my writing journey.

Here's what I learned about each thing on this list:

I wanted to write for fun and outlining felt like work

I thought that if writing wasn't fun all the time, then it would kill the joy of it for me. But writing a book with or without an outline is going to take work. Yes, it's a fun kind of work, but it's still work.

No matter how you write your book, it's likely going to take you a lot of time. And few writers want to spend a hundred hours writing something to never have it connect with readers.

The secret to life is that working for the things you want is worthwhile—too many people think it's not, but that feeling of finishing a book or seeing it published or getting 5-star reviews on it is priceless. You never get to feel that unless you do the work.

I realized I wanted to have fun but I also wanted the result of writing—a finished book that I could be incredibly proud of and feel good about sharing with others. Sharing my work was a big part of the fun of doing it to begin with!

I didn't think I could be imaginative or inspired if I outlined first

I thought that putting the actual words on paper or the screen was the inspiring part… but ironically,

I didn't start writing a lot of those words until after I learned to outline. Writer's block and the fear and anxiety of staring at a blank page were real for me. The less of an outline I had, the more likely I was to procrastinate on writing.

I eventually learned why this was. Mystery = Fear. Fear = Resistance. Resistance = Procrastination. Once I learned to take the mystery out of what I was about to write, I actually felt more inspired and imaginative… and I actually did the writing, too!

I also quelled my anxiety while writing, because I knew that the quality of my output would be stronger. I had already done some of the heavy lifting in the outline, and it comforted me to know that my efforts were producing something real, that could actually be read and enjoyed later.

I wanted to be the artist, not the business person

I believed that outlining was not very artistic, but over time I came to realize that outlining helped me be more artistic. If you want to be an artist, you likely want to spend most of your time creating, not trying to edit or rewrite your story to fix plot holes and dozens of poor choices in every chapter.

A book is made up of at least a thousand small decisions, and you're unlikely to get them all right in the first or even fifth draft. In truth, you're either going to fix your story before you write it or fix it after.

By outlining, I was able to significantly cut down on my editing time, which was such a relief as I didn't enjoy the editing process much.

I didn't think story structure was a part of my writing process

I felt attracted to a challenge like NaNoWriMo because I truly believed that getting my butt-in-chair and getting the words down was all I really needed to do. Story structure? That wasn't a part of my writing process!

I learned that story structure is a part of every writer's process, regardless of whether the writer outlines or not. The real question was, will I fix the story before I start writing it, or will I fix the story in a dozen rounds of edits after I've written it?

I found it much easier to fix the story before I had done all the drafting work. This kept me from going down random paths for tens of thousands of words that would eventually get cut anyway. I also found that continuity errors and lack of emotional resonance added up quickly, and it was much harder for me to find and replace all of that than to just never write it into the book to begin with.

I worried that outlining would make the story feel boring while writing it

I'm the type of person who hates spoilers and avoids them at all costs. So why would I spoil my own story before writing it?

I learned that writing an outline didn't mean that the drafting process had to be boring. First, the outline could be as detailed or not as I wanted. I also didn't have to stick to the outline if it wasn't working—the outline was really just a battle plan, but it could change as I went along. Finally, I learned that many writers did just that on purpose! They wrote the outline of just the first part of their book, then wrote that section, then wrote an outline for the second part of the book, and so on. My process could be whatever I wanted and whatever worked for me. That's why I encourage you to skip around in this book and do the lessons you want in the order that resonates with you!

I didn't want to outline in a logical or linear structure as it felt like the opposite of creativity

I'm a, "let's make this an art project" kind of person. I found outlining materials stodgy, boring, and schoolish. But your outline can look however you want as there are many ways to organize data. I found myself organizing my novels with color-coded notebooks and binders and through bullet journaling layouts, mindmapping, and flashcards. If you get any of my workbooks, including the Novel Writing Prep Companion Workbook, you'll see that these visual data tools drive many of my layouts—plus I include lots of thematic artwork to color in while you're thinking!

I worried about the time that outlining took and wondered if I was better served writing words

I thought that outlining was a waste of time and possibly a way to procrastinate on writing the actual words. I was bothered that there was no clear reward, like seeing the word count on my draft go up and up. But I found that outlining helps the writing part go much faster and made my production process more predictable.

Outlining also helped my larger writing process by significantly cutting down my editing and revising time. I never had to rewrite big chunks of my book or cut tons of chapters.

Finally, it also kept me from writing an unsalvageable draft, which is the biggest time waster of them all. In independent publishing, it means either never publishing the book or publishing a book that doesn't sell. In traditional publishing, it means never getting an agent for the book. Outlining saved me a ton of wasted effort and embarrassment.

I felt justified in not outlining because [insert successful author here] doesn't outline or *never* outlined and did just fine

I thought that if a successful author didn't have to outline, I didn't either. But that's a bit like saying if a world-renowned baker can bake without a recipe, I can produce a first-class souffle by banging a few pots and pans together too!

Successful authors have a strong internalization of story structure that is gained from writing dozens if not hundreds of books over a lifetime. Now that I've been teaching the work for awhile and worked with thousands of readers and students in my books and courses, I've seen that few if any writers start with a killer instinct for story—and even if they do, it must be nurtured.

Successful authors work very hard at their craft and professional authors who depend on their book royalties write outlines to speed their productivity. Don't be fooled by what random writers say online, as some people's advice is worth significantly more than the rest.

If you continue to write, you'll likely be able to scale back your outline over time, especially as you specialize in certain genres.

All of these false beliefs were holding me back from succeeding at my dream of becoming a full-time fiction author.

MY FIRST 4-FIGURE MONTH

Although my understanding of story was shifting, things didn't happen overnight. I struggled to apply what I was learning to my already written novel. The story was so strong in my mind, and I didn't have enough distance or enough know-how to fix the problems. I was largely trying to learn a new writing skill and do expert-level editing on my book, which didn't work.

Luckily, I kept myself afloat through freelance writing which allowed me to work from home and coffee shops. That marketing start-up job was my last full-time salaried job, and I've never looked back with even a twinge of regret, even though things did get challenging financially at various points.

I did have a few major wins along the way. I wrote a second book, a YA cyberpunk science fiction, and garnered over 100 reviews 4 stars and above. I realized I understood how to apply my digital marketing skills to my books, which was cool. I also learned how to write fast (the full story of which is in Write Better, Faster) and started a pen name to practice. Between my many projects, I was producing more books and building a catalog.

Eventually, though, I needed to make money with fiction. Specifically, I wanted to have a 4-figure month (at least $1000 US dollars made from fiction in a single month) so I could prove to myself and my new boyfriend that the time and effort I was putting into

WHY I WROTE NOVEL WRITING PREP

this was worthwhile. Enter National Novel Writing Month!

I completed my first NaNoWriMo in 2013, writing the first 50,000 words of the first two serials of a new series under my practice pen name. I made sure to write in a specific trope around romance to a billionaire, and the series took off. From there, I wrote about five serialized books in short succession, about one every month or two, and began earning about $1000 a month through royalties in mid-2014. I did it!

This was enough to get me motivated to keep going. It had been a long road to becoming a full-time author, with so many ups and downs, but I had the proof now that I could make money doing exactly what I loved. Since then, I have written over 30 books and, aside from a stint of burnout, made a moderate full-time income from my writing without taking on freelance clients.

The lessons I've included in this book were integral to my success with NaNoWriMo and beyond. In writing stories that were completely out of my niche, I learned to write-to-market quickly. Detailed outlining was absolutely necessary to my success so that I could easily shape my story as I was writing and make sure it was hitting reader expectations.

I can honestly say that I love the work I do every single day because it's entirely mine—my ideas, my vision, and my hard work to bring it to fruition. The first step for me and when my author career really began to take off was when I learned to write great stories quickly, which is exactly what this 30-day planner offers you.

HOW TO GET THE MOST OUT OF THIS BOOK

Novel Writing Prep is a great book on its own and you can completely outline your novel using just the book. I've also put together some companion resources in case they are helpful to you:

The Novel Writing Prep Challenge

I run a free 30-day challenge with all the content of this book three times a year: October, March, and June. If you want to join these challenges (videos, community, social updates, inspiration) you can check out the latest iteration here:

» **https://theworldneedsyourbook.com/nwp-challenge**

The Novel Writing Prep Companion Workbook and Companion Deck

The *Novel Writing Prep Companion Workbook* is a collection of workbook pages that follow the thirty days of outlining in this book. It's 200+ pages of bullet journal style layouts in 8.5" x 11" letter sizing. It's ideal for writers who love visual data organization or love getting creative with colors and art supplies. The book also doubles as a coloring book of sorts, with lots of line art that you can color in, allowing you to meditate as you percolate on your outline.

The *Novel Writing Prep Companion Deck* is a square card deck with each of the questions for all thirty days. You can do a daily card reading for your book edits, pull one and reflect on it if you like to skip around in the material, or use the cards like flashcards to remind yourself of important concepts after reading. You can also stick these to a board or wall in your house or in your favorite notebook to create your own visual layout. (If you do this, send pictures, please!) The card deck can also be used with the other decks for other books in *The Productive Novelist* series.

You can learn more about how to grab your own copies of these two resources at:

» **https://theworldneedsyourbook.com/novel-writingprep/**

The Finish Your First Draft Course

The Finish Your First Draft course is 10 video lessons that help you get to the end of your draft with a mix of content around outlining, writing habits, and drafting. If you are struggling to finish your first draft, this course can get you back on track and help you cross the finish line.

Learn more at:

» https://theworldneedsyourbook.com/shop

The Productive Novelist Series

The Productive Novelist series has 14 books spanning many independent publishing topics, including outlining, writing, editing, publishing, marketing, selling, business, strategy, and mindset. You can read the books in order or skip around based on where you're at in your writing and publishing journey.

Learn more about *The Productive Novelist* series here:

» https://theworldneedsyourbook.com/books

30 Days—Let's Go!

Day 1
IDEA TO CONCEPT

A lot of stories start with an idea—but usually, there's not enough there to begin writing a story.

Today we're going from idea to concept. Here are a few examples of ideas that eventually became stories in our modern culture:

- Two powerful wizards who battle it out for control of both the magic and muggle worlds
- A group of friends in their 20s-30s living in New York City
- Two male vampires fall in love with the same human girl

All of these ideas are extremely popular stories in today's culture, and two of them have spawned multiple franchises. What does this mean? Is there value in an idea alone if it can spawn multiple huge franchises, none of which are infringing on another's copyright?

More on that in a minute.

We don't need to think much about an idea or even define it fully; we just need to recognize that it is not a concept. If we can do that, then we can take an idea and hone it into more!

Moving beyond an idea, the concept is the hook of your story. It can usually be phrased as a "What if?" question, and it often points to a theme and/or conflict for the story. For example:

- An 11-year old child learns that he is a famous and celebrated hero in an underground magical world he never knew existed until now (*Harry Potter and the Philosopher's/Sorcerer's Stone*)

- 24 impoverished teenagers battle to be the lone survivor of the yearly Hunger Games, ensuring their status and wealth for the rest of their lives. (*The Hunger Games*)

- A teenage girl falls in love with a vampire who wants to kill her anytime he catches a whiff of her blood. (*Twilight*)

A concept isn't specific and usually doesn't "name names" or provide detail on the characters, the setting, or anything else. It may hint at those things, and it will certainly hint at conflict. But for the most part, it's a marketing piece that sums up the most basic

DAY 1: IDEA TO CONCEPT

design of the story.

In scriptwriting, it might be called a log line or a pitch. At a writer's conference, it might be the sentence you say when someone asks you what your book is about.

It is different from an idea because it's much more detailed, usually highlighting a few different elements:

- The protagonist
- The opposition (not necessarily the antagonist, but an opposing force)
- The "situation" (which is usually some sort of setting that forces the protagonist to meet his or her opposing force)

Larry Brooks, author of *Story Engineering*, describes a concept as something that launches a series or franchise. For example, what's a show about a group of friends in their 20s-30s living in New York City (the idea)?

If you said *Friends*, you're right. But if you said *How I Met Your Mother*, you're also right. What about *Girls*? *Seinfeld*? *Sex and the City*? *Gossip Girl*? *Baby Daddy*? *Don't Trust the B---- in Apartment 23*? Each of these series is the same in idea, but slightly different in concept.

The difference is the "What if?" part.

- What if a woman leaves her fiancé at the altar and seeks solace in her high school best friend, whom she hasn't spoken to in years? (*Friends*)

- What if a man tells his kids about how he met their mother, but starts the story long before he even meets her to explain why she was perfect for him? (*How I Met Your Mother*)

- What if a girl moves to New York City to be a "Carrie Bradshaw" type of writer, and finds out that it's nowhere close to the *Sex and the City* dreams she aspired to? (*Girls*)

We've now gone from the same idea to three unique concepts. Each of these is a "twist" on an old idea.

PROMPTS

Question #1: What is your book idea?

The first step is to write your book idea out in all its messy glory.

If you are struggling with this part, just ask yourself some additional questions.

What do I know about my book already?

Who is in it?

What is the first thing that happens in your book?

Question #2: Who is your protagonist?

At this point, we only need to know the barest basics about your protagonist. Specifically, you'll want to know gender, age (a rough narrowing to the appropriate decade of life is fine), and a handful of key relationships (but only if related to the conflict of your story).

Question #3: Who or what is your antagonistic force?

Your antagonistic force can be a person (called the antagonist) or anything else that opposes or stands in the way of your protagonist getting what he or she wants.

Question #4: What is the conflict between these two opposing sides?

For this question, we look at the conflict, which is a critical part of any hook.

If you are struggling to see the conflict between the protagonist and antagonistic force, you can ask yourself some additional questions.

What does the protagonist want that he/she doesn't get?

How is the protagonist blocked?

Question #5: What is the "what if?" summary sentence for your book?

Now is the moment of truth: what is the "what if?" summary sentence for your book?

If you're feeling stuck on this, look at some of the examples I've already given and switch out the protagonist, antagonist, and conflict for your own story.

It's not important to get this perfect. At this stage, we just want to have something to work from in this spot. Let it be messy for now!

Question #6: How is this a twist on a familiar story already in your genre?

Almost all concepts are a twist on genre tropes and conventions. This is possible without infringing on copyright because the answer to "what if?" is different each time.

For example, what's a television show about two male vampires who fall in love with the same human girl?

Go back to the "What if?" question:

- What if the two male vampires are close, and one sired the other? What if one ranks higher in that the other in vampire politics, and has ordered the lower-ranked one to start a relationship with the human in order to spy on her? (*The Southern Vampire Mysteries* and *True Blood* franchise)

- What if the two male vampires were estranged brothers? What if the human girl looked just like the woman who originally tore the brothers apart? What if all three were teenagers living in the same town? (*The Vampire Diaries* novels and television show)

In fact, if you wanted to broaden this idea, you would find many movies, books, television shows, and more that are basically a supernatural love triangle. *Twilight*, for example, fits this idea as well, except one of the males is a werewolf.

Keep drilling down on the question "What if?" to get to the root of what makes your story different (but similar) to what's already out there in your genre.

FEELING STUCK?

It's hard to explain exactly how to write a concept, and I've found that the best way to do so is to simply try writing concepts for your favorite books, television shows, and movies. It's much easier to write a concept for someone else's story, and that will give you practice for your own.

Look for ideas that translate to concepts and vice-versa. Again, this is really easy to do in television and movies. For example, *Friends With Benefits* and *No Strings Attached* are basically the same movie that came out a few months apart, and *Chasing Liberty* and *First Daughter* are basically the same movie that came out a few months apart, and on and on. You probably know books in your own genre that are similar to yours, so knowing how to distinguish them in concept will help set your work apart.

Additionally, don't get too hung up on the specific sentence. You are only trying to prep your novel, not pitch it to agents, publishers, or readers (at least not at this point). The sentence only matters to bring you clarity; no one else will see it!

Finally, if you have more information that the single concept sentence, feel free to brain dump it onto the page. The more you know about your book, the better! And if you don't have much beyond this first sentence, not a problem—we have 29 more days to flesh out your book.

Day 2
THEME

Today we are going to explore theme, which I believe is the heartbeat of any book. My Story Symmetry Framework is heavily based on finding the theme of your book and symbolically representing it throughout your book.

The easiest way to go from concept to theme is to ask, what does my main character represent?

Let's go back to a few of the concepts I listed before:

HARRY POTTER AND THE PHILOSOPHER'S/SORCERER'S STONE

> **Concept:** An 11-year old child learns that he is a famous and celebrated hero in an underground magical world he never knew existed

until now

Character Representation: Harry Potter represents good, love, while his nemesis (and the antagonist) Voldemort represents evil, fear.

Theme: It's a classic tale of good and evil, or love vs. fear.

THE HUNGER GAMES

Concept: 24 impoverished teenagers battle to be the lone survivor of the yearly Hunger Games, ensuring their status and wealth for the rest of their lives.

Character Representation: Katniss Everdeen represents childhood, innocence, victim of the games, while her nemesis The Capitol (and President Snow) represents coldness, cruelty, power, and lack of compassion.

Theme: It's about war and its effects on the children who fight it.

GAME OF THRONES AND A SONG OF ICE AND FIRE

Concept: The death of a king's mentor sets in motion a power struggle for his throne amongst the wealthiest families in his kingdom

Character Representation: There are no clear protagonists and antagonists, but everyone is trying to gain power with either good or evil

> intent.
> **Theme:** It's about the struggle for power and how much damage it causes while producing very little.

PROMPTS

Question #1: What is your concept?

If you have this from Day 1, rewrite it here (feel free to update it now that you've had time to think a little).

If you haven't created your book concept yet, have a look at the Day 1 lesson again!

Question #2: What do your protagonist and antagonist (or antagonistic force) represent?

If you have multiple characters that could fit these labels, feel free to list out each of them with a short description of what each represents to you.

Note that many themes can be laid out as some version of good versus evil or love versus fear, but not all. For example, in *The Fault in Our Stars*, it's ultimately a love story.

Love stories have two main characters, and the antagonistic force is whatever is keeping them apart (in this case, cancer).

You could say the theme is "cancer sucks," but take a minute to go deeper with it.

The theme for *The Fault in Our Stars* is around

death and what happens to you after you die. Are you a grenade who needs to lessen the impact of her death by staying contained and unattached (Hazel)? Do you feel you need to leave a legacy to make your life matter (Augustus)?

The resolution of that theme is that a short life can still be a good life. "Some infinities are bigger than other infinities."

What do your characters represent?

Question #3: What topics are you interested in?

If you are feeling unsure of your characters, perhaps start with your topics of interest. What matters to you? What is important in this world? Who do you wish you could help more? What do you wish you could say to the world?

Is there a way to create characters who represent and protagonist and antagonistic force around this topic?

Question #4: What are the main worldviews for this topic?

Most major topics have several different "camps." Take war, for example. You can probably think of at least a few different opinions on the topic!

If you were writing a book that included an war storyline, it would make sense to know the viewpoints of several people and create characters in the story who represented different viewpoints. These characters will approach war differently, and allowing them to interact with one another will be the basis for conflict in your story.

Who do you need to add to your story, given any complexities around your theme?

Question #5: What are the largest conflicts of opinion within this topic?

When it comes to theme, the more heated your theme is, the better. This will cause huge conflict between groups and characters within your story, since the theme persists through all the layers of the Story Symmetry Framework.

For example, in *The Hunger Games*, Katniss ultimately opposes war but is willing to go to war and kill when her life is threatened. Gale, on the other hand is a proponent of war and wants to defeat the enemy. He wants change through weapons, attacks, and killings. President Snow wants to avoid war at all costs and is willing to perpetuate the Hunger Games, believing that a small sacrifice will keep the colonies in fear and suppress revolts. For Peeta, war is very personal. He'll do what he must for the people he loves, but overall he is soft, kind, trusting, and hopeful for the future.

How can you turn up the heat on your theme? How can you diversify your characters' worldviews around the theme?

FEELING STUCK?

You may not have a theme just yet, or you may have too many themes and are having a hard time choosing. Be aware that your themes will emerge over time. You can keep coming back to this lesson to update it as you discover new theme ideas, as well as groups and characters that represent your theme.

You could also just pick something. Ultimately, we like to keep things aligned with theme. You don't have to do this to write great novels; however, it could help to have a true North. Decide on your true north and let other pieces of your book fall into place easily.

Let's keep going! 28 more days to flesh out your book.

Day 3
WORLDVIEWS

Now that you know your theme or hot topic, it's time to consider all the different sides of the issue.

BASEBALL EXAMPLE

For example, if you were to take a fairly charged topic, like whether the St. Louis Cardinals are going to win the World Series this year, there are a few major schools of thought:

- Yes, the Cardinals will win the World Series
- No, the Cardinals will not win the World Series
- Not sure

In those three general schools, there will be different approaches and viewpoints:

- In the Yes category, there will be die hard fans

who always think the Cardinals are going to win. There will be lots of fans who think it's more of a maybe but will say yes when asked. There will be analysts who are fairly impartial, who will be looking at the stats. There will be people who live in St. Louis and have just become fans, swept up in the excitement.

- In the No category, there will be people who hate the Cardinals because of [fill in the blank]. You could spin on that one for awhile—every reason is a new thread. There will be Cubs fans who will say no just for the sake of the rivalry. There will be the opposing team's fans who believe their team is going to win.

- In the Not Sure category, there will be people who don't follow baseball and have no idea who the Cardinals are. There will be people who do follow baseball but don't feel comfortable making a prediction. There will be people who live outside of the United States so it doesn't affect them. There will be people who just don't care for a variety of reasons—baseball bores them, they are only casual viewers, their team is out of the playoffs so they stopped following, they are in a challenging career or just had a baby, so they haven't followed the season this year, and so on.

Now, your theme threads look like this:

DAY 3 : WORLDVIEWS

- Yes, the Cardinals will win the World Series
    - Die hards
    - Maybe, but says yes
    - Analysts looking at the stats
    - Sunny-day fans
- No, the Cardinals will not win the World Series
    - Cubs fans
    - Pirates fans
    - Braves fans
    - Etc.
    - Haters
- Not sure
    - Don't follow baseball/sports
    - Don't count chickens before they hatch
    - Baseball is boring
    - Team out of playoffs, thus don't care
    - Haven't followed season this year
    - Outside the US, thus don't follow/care

These threads are the basis on which we'll create our groups and characters.

PROMPTS

Question #1: What is your worldview on your theme?

You likely have your own view of your theme and it's important to acknowledge that and look at which characters match your view and which don't.

Knowing this will also help to ensure you create lots of characters who don't quite share your view.

How can you tweak your own view to create multiple "good" characters?

How can you consider other views to create shades of grey characters across the larger issues?

Question #2: What is your protagonist's worldview on your theme?

Often, this will match your own worldview, but it doesn't have to. Additionally, your protagonist may not know his or her ultimate worldview and may discover it as the book goes on.

It helps to know where your protagonist might end up, though you don't have to decide now. Knowing how they feel at the beginning of the book is good enough for the moment!

Question #3: What is your antagonist's worldview on your theme?

Your antagonist's view should be opposing to your protagonist. After all, they'll have to battle it out to find resolution at the end of the book!

Question #4: What are all the different worldviews on your theme?

Have a quick brainstorm and see if you can come up with a list similar to my list about whether the Cardinals will win the World Series this year.

FEELING STUCK?

Are you feeling overwhelmed by the many worldviews a person might have on a particular topic? You don't need to explore every worldview.

For example, *The Fault in Our Stars* only heavily explores a few worldviews on the topic of death.

Likewise, some characters can share the same basic worldview. For example, in the *Harry Potter* series, both Harry and Ron think Hermione's desire to make S.P.E.W. a protest is silly. They share the same worldview, but Ron speaks out against it much more and Harry is often silent on the matter while continuing to do what he wants.

If you are feeling stuck on worldviews, it's okay to skip this lesson and move on. Worldviews, like theme, tend to emerge as you learn more about your

characters and the situation you are in.
27 days left!

Day 4
GROUPS

Once you have a strong idea of your theme and worldviews, you are ready to create Groups and Characters.

As you might have guessed, you already have—your groups correspond to the major schools of thought regarding your theme, while the shades of grey per school correspond to different characters you are going to create.

BASEBALL EXAMPLE

If you were writing a fiction book about baseball, you would have three different groups corresponding to the category above. You would create characters across the whole range—people who are die-hards, people who are active Cards haters, and people (probably the majority) who have other priorities or no investment in the outcome of the series. It might look something like this:

- **Group #1 -** Yes, the Cardinals will win the World Series
    - Character #1 - Die hards
    - Character #2 - Maybe, but says yes
    - Character #3 - Analysts looking at the stats
    - Character #4 - Sunny-day fans
- **Group #2 -** No, the Cardinals will not win the World Series
    - Character #5 - Cubs fans
    - Pirates fans
    - Braves fans
    - Etc.
    - Character #6 - Haters
- **Undecideds -** Not sure
    - Character #7 - Don't follow baseball/sports
    - Baseball is boring
    - Character #8 - Don't count chickens before they hatch

- Team out of playoffs, thus don't care
- Haven't followed season this year
- Character #9 - Outside the US, thus don't follow/care

Remember, you don't need a character for every worldview and you can combine any worldviews you come up with to fit the number of characters in your story. Play with this and figure out what works for you.

In *Veronica Mars*, which is about income disparity between the poor and the rich, and the corruption that comes with it, there are clear groups that represent all sides of the issue:

- The O'Niners, which is the rich class. It consists of Duncan Kane, Logan Echolls, and a slew of others. Veronica was once friends with this group of kids due to her father's place in the community as the sheriff.

- The Others, which is the lower income class. (Veronica insists that there is no middle class—"If you go [to Neptune High], your parents are either millionaires or your parents work for millionaires.") This group consists of Veronica, Wallace, Mac, and others.

- The PCH Gang, which is the "criminal" element of the show. The PCH Gang takes power and frequently riles up the Sheriff's department. They fight against the O'Niners.

- The police force, which is largely corrupt, now that Keith Mars is gone. Veronica Mars frequently attempts to manipulate them for information on her case of the week.

Each group represents different interests in the issue. The O'Niners represent privilege, the regular kids represent the lower income class or the victims of corruption, and the bicycle gang represents a darker and more rebellious side of the lower/middle class. The police force represents the larger corruption that happens when the two different groups are treated vastly differently.

That said, none of these groups is homogeneous. Within the O'Niners, there are jerks, nice people, truly terrible and corrupt people, and people who just happen to be wealthy. In the bicycle gang, Weevil, their leader, is generally a good guy who sometimes gets into trouble due to his circumstances. On the police force, Veronica actually at one point dates Leo D'Amato, one of the nicer Sheriff's Deputies—even though she generally thinks the whole group of them are idiots.

The group may have a general inclination, but there will (and should) always be shades of grey within any group. This adds depth to the theme and worldbuilding. (And no—worldbuilding is not just for fantasy and science fiction! We'll get to that on a later day.)

PROMPTS

Question #1: When you group different worldviews together, what cohorts do you get?

Try to organize your worldviews by similarity. Ideally, your different worldviews congregate around the protagonist and antagonist. This makes it easy to come up with secondary characters that these two characters can become allies with.

Question #2: How do you want to name each cohort?

Think about how you want to name various cohorts in your book and if possible, try to come up with clever names. For example, in the *Harry Potter* series, the name Slytherin plays on slithering like a snake, while Ravenclaw plays on sharp, a synonym for intelligent. In *Veronica Mars*, the O'Niners is a reference to the zip code the rich kids live in.

Question #3: What are the downsides of each group's worldviews?

What are the weaknesses for each group? For example, in *The Hunger Games*, District 2 was known for its wealth among the non-Capitol districts and its ability to turn out warrior tributes, but it also sided with the Capitol during the war and saw the majority of its people wiped out. By aligning with the Capitol, the rest of the districts felt distrust and disloyalty, even though all 12 districts were in the same predicament.

It's important to know the downsides for each group, as that can spur lots opportunities to win and lots of conflict and loss for various characters in that group throughout the book.

FEELING STUCK?

What works for your novel?

The *Harry Potter* series has four houses that each represent different traits one might have (while not encompassing all traits):

- Gryffindor - Bravery
- Slytherin - Self-Preservation
- Ravenclaw - Intelligence
- Hufflepuff - Kindness

Within each house, there are variations among the characters, though all Gryffindors tend to exhibit bravery, all Slytherins tend to exhibit self-preservation, and so on. For the most part, however, the groups are somewhat homogeneous while still maintaining a variety of characters in each. You as the reader are meant to root for Gryffindor and dislike Slytherin.

In *A Song of Ice and Fire*, the main characters are separated into 7 kingdoms and numerous houses or allegiances to houses. In this series, each character is distinct and unpredictable in terms of what he or she will do for his house or against his house. Allegiances shift, good and evil is a grey area, and relationships and loyalty are complicated. Because all the characters operate in shades of grey, you are not meant to root for any specific house, and no house could be attributed to simplistic terms like "good" or "evil."

You can create groups with lots of shading or groups that are more firm in their stance on life.

Finally, keep in mind that if you are writing a simpler story, like *The Fault in Our Stars*, you may not need groups at all and may want to just stick to characters.

26 days to go!

Day 5
CHARACTERS

Today, we're taking the groups we've just created and putting more characters in them. You may have already started doing this in previous days. If not, now is your chance!

A group may have a general view, but that doesn't mean the characters within the group are homogenous in their views and beliefs.

Like a political party, there are factions within the group, often with their own leaders. There are people who do what their told, even if it's questionable, and there are people who stand up for what they believe in. There are people who are in between, who will mostly do what their told but will "switch sides" when asked to do something that they feel crosses the line.

You want to have different shades of characters in each group to represent a solid range of the "spectrum" of whatever your issue might be.

From there, it's your choice on how you resolve the conflict, and in many ways your groups and characters become a symbol for the meaning of your story.

For example, in the *Harry Potter* series, I don't think this is a spoiler to say that Harry Potter ultimately defeats the bad guy (after tons of trials and tribulations). The series is thus saying that good will trump evil and love will trump fear. This is not a huge surprise, as most children's books would want to teach kids what society considers "good" traits and behaviors.

You can use characters to show a choice that the protagonist must make. This is a common trope in young adult fiction. Because these stories are typically coming of age, this often presents as a girl choosing between two suitors that each represent different life path choices for her. That's why every young adult novel has the love triangle.

The most prominent example of this is in the *Twilight Saga*, where Bella must choose between a life with the vampires or a life with the werewolves, technically shapeshifters. (These two groups are represented more specifically as a choice between Edward or Jacob).

These groups hate each other, and each represents something different to Bella Swan:

- **Vampires** - dangerous to humans, killers, but

can be redeemed if they go vegetarian

- **Shapeshifters** - defenders of humans, willing to go to war if necessary, no tolerance for bloodshed of any kind

Bella could have either of these lives, but she chooses Edward—who in my opinion, represents redemption.

Why is the third love interest, Michael, in the mix? Bella has this third suitor because her love choices are an extended metaphor, and Michael represents her human life... which she thoroughly rejects very early on in the books. She does not want to live the ordinary life. It's clear to the reader that her real choice is between vampires and shapeshifters, each of which Bella acknowledges has its positives... whereas her human life does not interest her much.

In *The Hunger Games*, Katniss must choose between Peeta and Gale. Gale is the fighter and Peeta is the lover—they are essentially foils of each other—and the question posed is does Katniss need a fighter or a lover?

She ultimately chooses Peeta because she doesn't want to be a part of war. Peeta softens her, reminds her of her humanity and what it means to live a life instead of fight for a cause. Katniss never fully embraces her place in the war, so this choice is no real surprise—Gale has a fire in him and will always fight for the cause.

PROMPTS

Question #1: What characters do you need to represent each of your groups and worldviews within each group?

Start to think about who these characters actually are, and if you are ready, start writing down things like gender, hair color, name, and more.

Question #2: Who is the leader of each of your groups?

Is there a leader? Is the group associated with the government or another larger body? What roles within the associated structure (e.g. government) should you include in your group?

Are there various factions within your groups, each with their own leader?

Question #3: What functions does each group fulfill within your story, and who leads each of the functions?

For example, do the groups recruit throughout the series and who handles that? Who do they recruit? How do they recruit? Does your protagonist get recruited?

Question #4: What other roles are needed within your group and who fulfills those?

In the *Harry Potter* series, Gryffindor also had a guard at the entrance (the Fat Lady), prefects (which included Percy Weasley), a Head Boy and Head Girl, a Quidditch captain, and a teacher head of house (Professor McGonagall).

While you don't need to name someone to every function, it's likely that your protagonist knows and interacts with the various roles within their group (if they have one).

Question #5: What characters does your protagonist need to help them choose a worldview?

If you are using characters to help represent a choice between two lifestyles or worldviews, you can name them here. Often, these characters are presented as a love triangle, but it doesn't have to be so.

In the movie *Batman Forever*, the Riddler tries to force Batman into choosing between saving Robin or his girlfriend. He asks, "Can Bruce Wayne and Batman ever truly coexist?"

Batman ends up saving both. "You see, I'm both Bruce Wayne and Batman, not because I have to be, now, because I choose to be."

FEELING STUCK?

DAY 5 : CHARACTERS

It can be a lot of work to create characters for each group within your story. If you have the framework, you can always add characters later or even purposely leave characters out of groups to be either loners on the fringes or still deciding. You can also create characters who seem to be part of one group, but are truly double agents.

Think of this effort as a loose container within which you can drop characters as needed.

We have 25 more days to go!

Day 6

CHARACTER RELATIONSHIPS

Another thing to think about as you are creating different characters in your groups is what your protagonist needs. We'll get into this in more detail when we discuss character arcs, but for now, you'll want to remember these to create a few characters to serve in these relationships with your protagonist:

- **Mentor(s) or Allies -** There are characters who help your protagonist face obstacles and overcome false beliefs. Not every protagonist needs a mentor or partner, but unless your character is James Bond and magically has every skill set he'll ever need, you probably want to create a few characters that make up for your protagonist's deficiencies.

- **Sidekicks -** These characters don't necessarily provide skill sets to your protagonist (though they could). Instead, they provide emotional support; they are your protagonists friends. You can certainly overlap this category with mentors, but it's also okay to have characters who just serve as friends in your story.

- **Love Interest(s)** - Few stories these days have zero romance, so don't forget to add a dash. Also, if you want to tie the romance to the theme, create a few love interests that each represent different choices for the protagonist. Love interests also serve as fantastic catalysts for a character to take action—particularly for men.

- **Family** - Similar to love interests, family can be a great catalyst or opposing force for a protagonist. Everyone has at least a mother and a father, so make sure you give your protagonist one of each. Siblings are important too! Unless your character must be an only child as a plot point or background story, I recommend providing a sibling or two.

Once you've defined these relationships for your protagonist, I recommend also defining them for your antagonist, even if we don't spend as much time with every single character you end of creating. You can use these categories that mirror the above:

- **Evil Mentor(s) (Sometimes called Contagonists)** - They contaminate the protagonist's mind and mess with his world view. A great example of this is Barty Crouch Jr. as Mad-Eye Moody in the *Harry Potter* series. These evil mentors are extensions of the antagonist but hurt the protagonist.

- **Henchmen** - Sidekicks for antagonists
- **Tempter/Temptress** - The equivalent of a love interest for the antagonist, who tempts the protagonist toward the "dark side." In *Homeland*, for example, this would be the war hero/terrorist that CIA agent Carrie Mathison is both sleeping with and investigating at the same time.

PROMPTS

Question #1: What characters have you already created that fit into these categories?

Can a current group member (potentially in the antagonist's group, even!) become your protagonist's mentor, sidekick, or love interest? How can this cause conflict or drive the story forward?

Try to match each of your different worldview characters to the role they play for the protagonist. Do you have characters that can serve your story in multiple ways?

Question #2: What gaps do you see in these categories?

The more characters you add (even by name), the more you shape your protagonist and the more believable your story becomes. You can also more easily come up with backstories, plot points, interactions, situations, problems, and solutions for your protagonist.

Question #3: If you've created any new characters, what groups do they belong to?

You can also answer questions about their worldviews, beliefs in relationship to the theme, relationships with each other and the protagonist, and more.

Question #4: What is the order and timing around introducing these characters to the narrative?

You may not know the answer to this for many characters yet, but for some you will. You can make some notes of when each character first appears and how each is introduced. This will allow you to space characters appropriately and also help you come up with scenes as you move along.

FEELING STUCK?

There's a lot to balance in your story at this point,

specifically with regard to characters.

Assuming you've finished up the lessons so far, you should have many, many characters populating your story now. This alone will give your story and characters more depth and conflict, simply because the real world is also made up of many, many people. Your story world is likely starting to feel more realistic at this point.

If you are struggling to come up with characters, or it doesn't make sense to create this many characters in your story, don't fret. You don't need to introduce all these characters at once, and it most likely wouldn't serve your narrative (or your reader) to do so anyway.

Keep this framework in mind and continue to add characters as needed. If you are feeling overwhelmed, you can come back to this lesson later and add more to it. You can also keep going and let the plot bring forward more characters.

On to Day 7—24 more days!

Day 7
CHARACTER FATAL FLAWS

As most storytellers know, main characters (specifically the protagonist) must move, grow, and change within a story. Similar to how we might define plot arcs, we call this growth throughout the story a character arc.

Your protagonist and any other point-of-view (POV) character needs a character arc for every book in your series.

Every character you expect to go through a transformation (or to have a character arc) needs to start with a fatal flaw. This fatal flaw is a way of looking at the world (could even be a worldview) that will change (or get resolved) by the end of the story. Here are several fatal flaws from popular modern stories:

- Harry Potter is afraid that he can't beat Voldemort; his fatal flaw is lack of confidence (*Harry*

Potter)

- Tyrion Lannister has been shunned by his family his entire life; his fatal flaw is he is desperate for love and approval from his father and sister (*A Song of Ice and Fire*)
- Katniss Everdeen doesn't want to bring children into this world because it's so terrible; her fatal flaw is she has no hope for the future (*The Hunger Games*)

These fatal flaws are the basis of the character arc. From the fatal flaw, you must now determine the transformation (if any) you want the character to go through. Here's what this (potentially) looks like for each of the fatal flaws above:

THE HARRY POTTER SERIES

Fatal Flaw: Harry Potter is afraid that he can't beat Voldemort; his fatal flaw is lack of confidence

Transformation: Harry Potter recognizes his strengths where Voldemort is weak and uses those to his advantage to beat him

A SONG OF ICE AND FIRE

Fatal Flaw: Tyrion Lannister has been shunned by his family his entire life; his fatal flaw is he is desperate for love and approval from his father and sister

Transformation: Tyrion finds love and approval somewhere else (perhaps within himself) and is satisfied with it

THE HUNGER GAMES

Fatal Flaw: Katniss Everdeen doesn't want to bring children into this world because it's so terrible; her fatal flaw is she has no hope for the future

Transformation: Katniss learns that although there are terrible people and happenings in the world, there is plenty that is worth fighting for.

As you can see from the examples, the fatal flaw is the thing that's going to ruin everything for the protagonist if he or she doesn't get it in check:

- Harry Potter needs to boost his confidence that he can beat Voldemort, or else he's going to die at his hand

- Tyrion Lannister does everything he can to win his father's approval (and to a lesser extent, his sister's) and they consistently stab him in the back or throw him under the bus, often in attempts to get him killed

- Katniss Everdeen becomes a symbol of freedom and justice against her will, putting a huge target on her back. She will die if she doesn't fight

The fatal flaw and the transformation serve as endpoints for the character arc. The fatal flaw belongs at the beginning of the book, while the transformation belongs at the end.

Once you have figured out your character's fatal flaw and transformation, we can construct the full character arc using the concept of false beliefs.

PROMPTS

Question #1: Which characters will have a full character arc in your book?

I recommend giving your protagonist and any other point-of-view characters (as long as those POV characters will be present throughout the text) a full character arc.

You may also want to know the antagonist's character arc, even if it happens off-screen or in backstory. At the least, you may want to know the antagonist's fatal flaw.

Question #2: For each character with a full character arc, what is their fatal flaw?

If you are struggling to come up with a fatal flaw, consider a simple question: what is most important to your character?

For example, for Katniss Everdeen from *The Hun-*

DAY 7 : CHARACTER FATAL FLAWS

ger Games, her sister Primrose Everdeen is the most important thing in her life. We learn this throughout the first chapter as she saves her sister from starving (multiple times) and then sacrifices herself in her sister's place in the Hunger Games.

Then ask yourself: what does this thing actually represent?

For Katniss, Primrose represents childhood innocence. Katniss believes in protecting children from the harsh conditions of the world she lives in.

In the games, this same childhood innocence is represented by another tribute named Rue, who is also only 12-years old, just like Katniss's sister.

You could extend this even further by looking at Katniss's backstory, which is that her own childhood ended at 11 years old when her father died, her mother checked out of life, and she became the sole provider for her family.

Seeing the pattern yet?

Katniss's fatal flaw is her deep desire for a world where children remain innocent, and her deep hopelessness over ever being able to create or even imagine that world. In fact, she says herself in the first chapter that she could never bring her own children into the world as a result of what she sees around her.

So what is most important to your character and what does that thing represent?

Question #3: What are some more ways you can represent your character's fatal flaw?

Harry Potter has a scar on his forehead, a symbol of his weakness to Voldemort.

Katniss immediately meets and attracts Rue, who reminds her of her sister Primrose, once she enters the games.

Bella receives a crescent-shaped scar on her hand as a reminder that Edward was able to battle his desire for her blood before he killed her. His love was stronger than his primal instincts, and she remained safe with him. The scar went on to be the center of the struggle through the rest of the series, where he wanted to protect her soul by keeping her a mortal human.

Question #4: How is the fatal flaw going to ruin everything for the character if he or she doesn't get it under control?

It is not easy for a character (or anyone) to overcome a fatal flaw, as a fatal flaw is always built on a cluster of false beliefs. This means that the character is going to resist the change he or she must make throughout the book. It will take a lot (usually a life or death situation) to push the character to change his or her beliefs. What does that look like for your character?

DAY 7 : CHARACTER FATAL FLAWS

Question #5: How does the character conquer the fatal flaw by the end of the story?

By the end of the *Hunger Games* trilogy, the war is over and Katniss has children of her own. She has overcome her false beliefs around hope for the future and the children (and the rest of her choices in the epilogue) represent that.

While you don't need to know the end game for your character just yet, it could be helpful.

Your book's ending will be most satisfying when it shows that your character has conquered his or her fatal flaw. Pay close attention to the three examples in this section. Each of these series were massively popular, and a big part of that was owing to having the fatal flaw spelled out at the beginning of the series, reiterated throughout the series, and resolved by the end of the series.

This doesn't just happen. It happens when the author thinks it through at the structural level. How will you see the fatal flaw through?

FEELING STUCK?

There are lots of characters who don't reach the transformation of their character arc. These unresolved character arcs are perfectly fine in genres like thriller or mystery or comedy, so don't worry if your character has no transformation at the moment.

If you are writing a standalone novel, in most cases you may as well give your protagonist some sort of transformation, even if it's small. You aren't planning on using the character again, so why not?

If you are writing a series, you can bring the character forward through a transformation, then in the next book bring them back to their original false belief (making it true for them again). This keeps the character at a baseline, never changing much in personality, beliefs, or status (married, single, rich, poor, etc.).

Dan Brown's *Robert Langdon* series, best known for its second book *The Da Vinci Code*, is a great example of this. Langdon rarely changes book to book and tends to wear roughly the same outfits, date roughly the same type of woman (usually someone intelligent that he meets on the case), and have roughly the same interests (art, architecture, puzzles, and symbolism).

In this example, Langdon still has a fatal flaw (claustrophobia) which serves as more of a Chekhov's gun throughout the series. He never gets over his fatal flaw book to book, and he almost always ends up in a situation that forces him to reconcile with his fears around tight spaces.

For Langdon, the fatal flaw is present and the end transformation is present (he usually solves the case, ends up with the woman, and writes another book or two about it), but they don't coincide.

This may fit your situation for your book, in which case you can model your fatal flaw and transformation off of this example.

DAY 7 : CHARACTER FATAL FLAWS

That's said, it will depend on genre for what is the right solution for you!

23 more days. Let's do this!

Day 8
CHARACTER FALSE BELIEFS

False beliefs are permutations of the fatal flaw. If the fatal flaw is the BIG thing your protagonist has wrong about his or her life, the false beliefs are the small truths that your protagonist holds dear. These small truths are holding your protagonist back from breaking through the fatal flaw.

HARRY POTTER'S FALSE BELIEFS

Harry's fatal flaw through the entire series is that he lacks confidence in his abilities to defeat Voldemort. It is expressed in his false beliefs, which he speaks and thinks frequently:

- He's not actually special or the "Chosen One."
- He was unluckily chosen at birth.

DAY 8 : CHARACTER FALSE BELIEFS

- He is like Voldemort/Tom Riddle. (They are both orphans, they both speak parseltongue, etc.)

- He only survives with the help of others.

- He often survives due to lucky circumstances (like being wand twins with Voldemort).

- He's destined to die at Voldemort's hand.

These are just a few I came up with off the top of my head, but you see them over and over again throughout that series. Many of these come out in the fifth book in the series, *Harry Potter and the Order of the Phoenix*, while he is explaining to Dumbledore's Army why they shouldn't admire his past encounters with Voldemort.

Here's a rough breakdown of how they show up in the books over and over again:

> **Book 1** - Harry fears that Voldemort is coming back for him. He's haunted by the confrontation between them when he was a baby, and the burden of being the "Chosen One." All he wants is be normal and have his parents back (as seen in the mirror of erised).
>
> **Book 2** - Harry fears that he will be like Tom Riddle/Voldemort. He sees a lot of similarities as he battles the Heir of Slytherin. It scares him!
>
> **Book 3** - Harry fears Sirius Black, the man

who gave his parents up to Voldemort. This goes back to the same false belief from book 1, that Sirius is coming after Harry, the "Chosen One," to finish off what he started.

Book 4 - Harry fears that he's not smart enough or good enough to compete against the older students and win the Triwizard Tournament. This mirrors how he feels he's not smart enough or good enough to beat Voldemort.

Book 5 - Harry fears death (thanks to Cedric Diggory, represented symbolically with the introduction of the thestrals). He is the reluctant leader of Dumbledore's Army, even though he doesn't see himself as a hero. He is running toward the prophecy (toward death at Voldemort's hand).

Book 6 - Harry fears his own judgement after the fiasco at the ministry of magic that got [spoiler] killed for no reason.

Book 7 - Harry fears that Dumbledore was wrong. Wrong to trust Snape, wrong to send Harry after the horcruxes instead of the hallows. Harry is afraid that Dumbledore's plan sucks and doubts whether he should follow it. This has nothing to do with Dumbledore—it's Harry's own judgment that he questions.

All of these fears (which he conquers one by one) are just permutations of the fatal flaw—that he lacks confidence to destroy Voldemort. They are the fatal flaw manifesting in different ways, different forms, not unlike they do in real life. Just as he conquers one of those fears, another one pops up in a slightly different permutation—just like in real life. (Have you heard the phrase, "New level, new devil," before?)

Your protagonist has a fatal flaw. But this fatal flaw lurks below the surface. It's not stated explicitly in the text, and the character isn't necessarily even aware of it. Your job is to represent it over and over again in the form of false beliefs, so that your characters can chip away at these throughout the story.

PROMPTS

Question #1: Look at your character's fatal flaw. What are some false beliefs that led him or her to believe or behave that way?

Make a list of whatever comes to mind. It doesn't have to be a perfect list or a complete list. What are some of the reasons your character believes what he or she believes?

Question #2: What false beliefs come from your character's backstory?

Look at the pivotal events in your character's childhood. Most of our wounding as humans comes from events that happened at a young age. Give your character a backstory that explains where he or she developed some of the false beliefs he or she currently carries.

Question #3: What false beliefs come from your character's environment?

Look at the place your character grew up in.
Look at the people your character grew up around.
Look at the family, teachers, and people of authority who might have influenced your character.
How did your character come to believe the things he or she believes?
What shaped their worldview?

Question #4: What false beliefs come from events that might happen in the story?

You may not yet know exactly what's going to happen in your story, and that's okay!

If you have any scenes already playing out in your mind, you can add them here and identify the false belief at the core of them.

For example, one of Bella's (and Edward's) false beliefs in *Twilight* is that she is safe once Edward proves he isn't going to kill her. Then, a vampire outside of Edward's family discovers her and desires to drain her blood.

This event shatters her false belief and by the end, makes her want to become a vampire even more.

If you've come up with any of these scenes or scenarios already, jot them down now—your effort will come in handy down the line!

Question #5: What is the truth behind each false belief?

False beliefs are not necessarily "false," but rather unbalanced beliefs.

For example, Harry is not wrong to believe he can't defeat Voldemort. In fact, he has lots of evidence that he can't, including multiple battles that he loses, multiple times that he is outsmarted, and multiple ways in which he is not willing to cross the lines that Voldemort has crossed to gather power.

At the same time, it's probably not a spoiler to say that he eventually does defeat Voldemort without compromising his values or being the stronger wizard.

Every trait you can think of comes with strengths and weaknesses. Hufflepuffs are nice but can easily be taken advantage of due to their willingness to give others the benefit of the doubt. Slytherins are self-preserving but can also be ambitious, shrewd, brilliant, and protective of the people they love.

In Harry's case, his humility is a strength. Voldemort underestimates him time and time again, and this is eventually his downfall.

Harry's loyalty and unwillingness to fight fire with fire is also strength. He rallies a large number of people to fight (and sometimes die) against Voldemort for him.

His love is a strength. He believes in people, forgives people, and saves people, even his long-time nemesis Draco Malfoy.

What is the strength behind the fatal flaw and false beliefs? How does each false belief protect the character and work for them?

And where do they need more discernment and balance?

FEELING STUCK?

Since false beliefs tend to be under the surface, subconscious, and hard for us (or our characters) to see, it may help to look at more examples. Look at books in your genre (or simply think of a few of your favorite books) and break down some of the false beliefs of the protagonist. Try to tie each false belief to a larger fatal flaw for that character.

If you are struggling to find the false beliefs around your character's fatal flaw, you can also simply skip this section and save it for later. We will have many more opportunities to look at false beliefs. It may be easier to start with plot (the external arc) and work your way backwards to identify the false belief (the internal arc) in each plot point. Then, you can check to see that it aligns back to the fatal flaw.

22 days left!

Day 9
CHARACTER MOTIVATIONS AND THE FATAL FLAW

Every protagonist has an internal and external conflict that must be overcome before reaching the transformation. These conflicts are expressed early on in the book through two devices, the motivation and the fatal flaw.

The motivation and fatal flaw are the external and internal conflicts, respectively. They are two acknowledgments of the same problem. The external plot arc kicked off by the motivation is symbolic of the internal character arc kicked off by the fatal flaw, and vice-versa.

THE FAULT IN OUR STARS

Character: Hazel Grace Lancaster
Fatal Flaw: Wants her loved ones to move on unharmed after her death

False Beliefs: She believes that her mother will no longer be a mother when Hazel dies (a comment she overheard accidentally at the hospital). She is obsessed with a book called *An Imperial Affliction* that ends mid sentence and longs to know what happens to the other characters. She doesn't want to start a relationship with Augustus Waters because she doesn't want to be like his last girlfriend, who died of cancer. She believes that she is a grenade and seeks to minimize the damage to those around her by not getting close to anyone.

Transformation: She realizes that her death may hurt others, but she can still have a full life, even if it's a short one. She learns that her parents' lives will go on after her death. She learns that her mother will always be a mother. She tells Augustus that "some infinities are bigger than other infinities" and that she's happy for the small infinity he has given her (their romance).

You can imagine that her fatal flaw is first revealed at the beginning of the novel, she breaks through her false beliefs in the middle of the novel, and she experiences a transformation at the end of the novel. But how do we create an actual plot from that?

We do this by defining her motivation from the fatal flaw and matching up the external and internal

DAY 9 : CHARACTER MOTIVATIONS

journeys.

Remember, the fatal flaw and motivation are two sides of the same coin.

In *The Fault in Our Stars,* Hazel's flaw is that she sees herself as a grenade.

Augustus challenges this right away, getting closer to her as they exchange messages and read each other's favorite books. Hazel discloses that she wants to know the ending to *An Imperial Affliction,* a book that ends mid-sentence when the protagonist dies. Augustus contacts the author, who says he will tell her in person if she comes to Amsterdam.

From this point on, Hazel makes a decision. She is going to learn the ending to *An Imperial Affliction,* no matter what it takes. This is her motivation for the rest of the book.

On the outset, the fatal flaw and motivation don't look like they go together... but for anyone who has read the book, we know that they do. Learning the ending to *An Imperial Affliction* is Hazel's way of reconciling her own death and belief that she is a grenade. She longs to know that her parents will be okay after she's gone. She want to know that they have a future, and she attempts to reconcile that by learning the futures of the other characters in *An Imperial Affliction.*

To be clear, *An Imperial Affliction* is a representation or symbol of Hazel's fatal flaw.

But why do we need the symbol?

Because a book does not move forward based on

a fatal flaw. As stated before, the fatal flaw is usually subconscious to the character. The character has no idea they are operating under a fatal flaw!

Hazel cannot say to herself, "I really need to get past my fear of what happens to my loved ones after I die." She cannot set out on that journey. She's just not that self-aware.

And if she was, well, there wouldn't be much of a story. If she knew that was her problem, she would then just go to her parents and ask them, "what's your plan for when I die?" They would tell her and that would be the end of the book as her transformation would be complete.

The motivation is critical. It is the rocket fuel behind entire book, and the thing that launches your protagonist on his or her quest.

PROMPTS

Question #1: What is the protagonist's quest?

If he or she doesn't have a quest just yet, what is a physical representation or symbol of the character's fatal flaw?

Question #2: How does the quest tie to the motivation?

How can you create a motivation that will launch the protagonist on a quest?

In some cases, like in *The Fault in Our Stars*, the mo-

DAY 9 : CHARACTER MOTIVATIONS

tivation is a metaphor. It doesn't have to be though.

In the *Harry Potter* series, the motivation is survival and peace, as most believe that Voldemort is still alive in some form and will come back for Harry. In the first book, this is represented by protecting the philosopher's stone, which is thought to have the power to bring Voldemort back into a human body.

In the *Twilight Saga*, the motivation is love and romance, as Bella and Edward fall in love. In the first book, this is represented by their burgeoning relationship and her desire to join the vampire world, despite what it means for her humanity and despite the dangers it holds. She's willing to do whatever it takes to be with Edward long-term, even if she has to die.

Question #3: How does the motivation reflect the fatal flaw?

For Harry Potter, much of the first book is spent building his confidence, which is his fatal flaw. He is trying to protect the philosopher's stone, which will prevent Voldemort from coming back (for the time being). Throughout the book, he goes through obstacle after obstacle, saving his friends and breaking through every challenge that the professors of Hogwarts use to protect the stone. By the end of the book, he learns a valuable lesson: while he isn't nearly as strong or as skilled at magic as Voldemort, he has strengths that may help him defeat Voldemort in the future.

The motivation to protect the philosopher's stone challenges his false beliefs and fatal flaw over and over again.

For Bella Swan in the *Twilight Saga*, Bella believes the love between Edward and her is worth every sacrifice. She sacrifices her friends, her family, her safety, and eventually her humanity to be with him eternally. Her initial motivation to be with Edward and join the vampire world goes straight back to her fatal flaw, which is that she's human, physically weak, and fairly helpless and in need of protection.

FEELING STUCK?

Remember that the fatal flaw and motivation are a mirrored pair, internal and external, respectively. If you have one, you can figure out the other.

If you're feeling stuck, can you decide on one or the other? This will move you forward.

And what if you have a fairly static character with a static fatal flaw?

Robert Langdon from *The Da Vinci Code* is afraid of tight spaces, but he is also so fascinated with mysteries and his area of expertise around symbolism that he is willing to put his life in danger to chase down ancient secrets and puzzles.

The motivation is truth, and it ties directly to the fatal flaw because the truth is going to challenge his greatest fear directly every time. Additionally, his search for truth always sends him on a quest, which,

DAY 9 : CHARACTER MOTIVATIONS

as a fairly mild-mannered professor, he is not always ideally equipped for.

We have 21 days left to go, which means we are almost a third done.

Press on, Igniter!

Day 10
CHARACTER GOALS AND THE FALSE BELIEFS

Just as the fatal flaw and motivation are twin concepts, two expressions of the same problem, the false beliefs and goals are also twin concepts, two expressions of the same solution.

The goal is just the external expression of the false belief, and the false belief is just the internal expression of the goal.

Each is a solution or coping mechanism for the fatal flaw/motivation.

When a false belief is challenged, the protagonist either reaffirms the belief or breaks through the belief.

Similarly, when a goal is challenged, the protagonist either succeeds at the goal or fails at it.

Whereas the fatal flaw and motivation stay the same throughout the story and are only broken through at the end, the false beliefs and goals change

DAY 10 : CHARACTER GOALS

and are broken through as we go along—primarily in the middle section of the story.

THE FAULT IN OUR STARS:

Character: Hazel Grace Lancaster
Fatal Flaw: Wants her loved ones to move on unharmed after her death
Motivation: Learn the ending to the other characters' futures in *An Imperial Affliction*
False Beliefs: She believes that her mother will no longer be a mother when Hazel dies (a comment she overheard accidentally at the hospital). She is obsessed with a book called *An Imperial Affliction* that ends mid-sentence and longs to know what happens to the other characters. She doesn't want to start a relationship with Augustus Waters because she doesn't want to be like his last girlfriend, who died of cancer. She believes that she is a grenade and seeks to minimize the damage to those around her by not getting close to anyone.
Transformation: She realizes that her death may hurt others, but she can still have a full life, even if it's a short one. She learns that her parents' lives will go on after her death. She learns that her mother will always be a mother. She tells Augustus that "some infinities are bigger than other infinities" and that she's

87

happy for the small infinity he has given her (their romance).

From this, we can map out goals that will directly help Hazel break through her false beliefs.

False Belief: She believes that her mother will no longer be a mother when Hazel dies (a comment she overheard accidentally at the hospital)
Goal: She wants to see her mother to have a life outside of her.
False Belief: She is obsessed with a book called *An Imperial Affliction* that ends mid-sentence and longs to know what happens to the other characters.
Goal: She wants to get the ending from the author directly, which requires her to go to Amsterdam.
False Belief: She doesn't want to start a relationship with Augustus Waters because she doesn't want to be like his last girlfriend, who died of cancer.
Goal: She pushes him away for as long as she can, keeping him firmly in the "crush" category.
False Belief: She believes that she is a grenade and seeks to minimize the damage to those around her by not getting close to anyone.
Goal: She closes herself off to anyone new so

DAY 10 : CHARACTER GOALS

  - that she doesn't break their hearts.

This list of goals is helpful, but in order to create a real plot that we can start writing, we need to put them in some sort of order.

There's a ton of wiggle room here, because you can break through these beliefs in any order.

That said, it may be helpful to move from least offensive false belief to most offensive false belief in your story, because the harder it is to overcome a false belief, the larger and more challenging the external goal would need to be.

Here's the rough order in which Hazel pursues these goals:

- She believes that she is a grenade and seeks to minimize the damage to those around her by not getting close to anyone. So she closes herself off to anyone new so that she doesn't break their hearts.

- She is obsessed with a book called *An Imperial Affliction* that ends mid-sentence and longs to know what happens to the other characters. So she wants to get the ending from the author directly, which requires her to go to Amsterdam.

- She doesn't want to start a relationship with Augustus Waters because she doesn't want to be like his last girlfriend, who died of cancer.

So she pushes him away for as long as she can, keeping him firmly in the "crush" category.

- She believes that her mother will no longer be a mother when Hazel dies (a comment she overheard accidentally at the hospital). So she wants to see her mother to have a life outside of her and finally confronts her about it.

Now we are starting to see a plot come together, which we will map out in order in a later lesson. For now, it's good to get a rough idea of how the character arc might play out, but there's still lots of room for rearrangement in the future.

Next, let's talk about how to move your character through these external goals to overcome their false beliefs. Here's how that works:

- If the character succeeds in her Goal, it confirms the false belief, which allows the character to continue believing it.

- If the character fails in her Goal, it challenges the false belief, which allows the character to break through.

Armed with that knowledge now, here's the rough order within which Hazel overcomes her false beliefs:

- She doesn't want to date Augustus at first, because he's already had one girlfriend die of cancer. She confronts him on this, telling him she's a grenade, to which he replies, "It would be a privilege to have my heart broken by you." She's unable to scare him off (failure). They eventually do have a relationship.

- She attempts to get the ending for An Imperial Affliction, but the author insists that the characters "simply cease to exist." Hazel is incredibly unsatisfied with this. She wants to imagine a future for the characters, who are a metaphor for her own parents and all the people she will leave behind when she dies. She never does get her ending (failure), but she realizes that her true goal is securing her own loved ones' futures.

- She confronts her mother about the comment she overheard, that she won't be a mother after Hazel dies. Her mother then tells her that she is taking classes and earning a degree and has plans for her life if and when Hazel passes away. This helps Hazel realize that even her death can't make her mother not a mother (failure). She is able to accept her death with the peace of mind that her family will continue on.

Hopefully, by now you can see how you can plot out your entire story, figuring out each of your major moments by simply lining up the false beliefs and choosing goals to either break through a belief or confirm a belief. This is how the character moves along through the story and makes progress toward the transformation.

PROMPTS

Question #1: Look at your list of false beliefs. Can you list them in order from easiest to break through to hardest to break through?

For this exercise, your ranking may feel arbitrary for now. That's because there is no right answer.

Trust your intuition and put those false beliefs in whatever order feels right for the moment.

You can definitely rearrange these false beliefs into a different order later (and we will be rearranging them as needed throughout the rest of this book).

Question #2: Look at your list of false beliefs, now organized. What are some external goals that could prompt success or failure at breaking through each false belief?

You may not be sure of the answers to this, but again, that's because there are no right answers.

Simply write down whatever comes to you through your intuition and your basic knowledge of your story.

We are making it up as we go along on purpose, and we will be rearranging later anyway, so it doesn't completely matter what you have down in this section for the moment.

Question #3: Look at your external goals. How does each tie back to the initial motivation?

For this question, your main goal is check in on alignment. As I've stated, alignment between all the elements of story is the key to a commercially successful story.

Thus far, we've gone from fatal flaw to false beliefs to motivation to goals. Each derived from the previous, one after the other. Thus, each goal should lead all the way back to fatal flaw through the motivation.

If you've done the lessons thus far, you should be able to answer this question easily for each goal.

If you find yourself getting stuck, there's no need to worry just yet. It could be that you are still weaving the threads of your story. We have more questions down the line that will help you get these into deeper alignment as you go along.

For the time being, if you see a misalignment between goals and the initial motivation (or the fatal flaw, or the false beliefs), ask yourself, "What can I change to bring these elements into alignment?"

It could be that you want to adjust or deepen the fatal flaw or change the motivation. You may want to find more false beliefs or come up with new goals.

See what you can do to get these into alignment sooner rather than later. Eventually, they will need to be in alignment. May as well bring them closer now!

Question #4: Can you map out some key points on your protagonist's quest, using the motivation and goals?

Here, we are getting closer to a loose outline of the plot of your story, based on the character's arc.

Note that you are not fleshing out the whole plot in this section. You are merely mapping out the plot points that will move your character forward.

Some plot points don't move the character forward, but instead move the plot forward.

So your loose outline will still have a lot of gaps that we'll be filling in in later sections.

Question #5: Can you map out some key points on your protagonist's character arc, using the corresponding fatal flaw and false beliefs?

If you can answer this question, you will have two things: your character arc or arcs, and the knowledge that your plot thus far is going to move your character through his or her respective arc.

This is a big deal! In ten days, you've gone from an idea to having a huge piece of your book (character journeys) loosely mapped out.

Everything is in alignment and you can breathe a sigh of relief that your book makes emotional sense thus far. Your most important characters are transforming throughout your book, which will please readers.

Well done!

FEELING STUCK?

What if you didn't do well when you hit question #5 of this lesson?

You still get to pat yourself on the back. Because even if you don't have full character arcs, you have the building blocks for them. And in the coming days, we will build out your character arcs from the external perspective through the lessons on plot.

Right now a plot is starting to thicken through the fatal flaw, false beliefs, motivation, and goals. You may be feeling overwhelmed at this point or you may feel like you've done it all "wrong," to which I would say slow down and stop worrying.

We'll be revisiting the plot and these concepts a few more times throughout this book, so you don't need to have everything figured out at the moment.

Write down what you know to the best of your ability, using the prompts you've learned thus far. You can't possibly miss anything or leave anything out at this point. Your novel is only growing from here—this is novel prep time!

I also want to assure you that if you are feeling confused, it's because we are currently accessing plot in a roundabout way that's not often taught. That's on purpose. We are looking at plot from its underlying emotional skeleton and getting those pieces into place as best as possible, before we cover them up with the actual plot of the book.

Think of it like building an actual human body. You aren't ever going to see your own skeleton (hopefully) but it's the reason that your body holds its form. With just a skeleton, you would look pretty unattractive and probably be dead. A skeleton is certainly not enough to be a body, and your current knowledge of your book is certainly not enough to be your novel.

But without the skeleton, your body doesn't work. It falls apart. And without the answers to these first ten days of prompts, your book doesn't work, either. It falls apart too.

This is because the emotional layer of your book (the characters' internal character arcs) is also the heartbeat of your book. The work you've done over the past ten days is the stuff that will make readers fall in love with your work at the subconscious level.

They will never see this work as they read the book (hopefully). You will cover up this layer and make all of it seem effortless and flowing.

But you as the author need to see this layer and put it in place for the sake of your book.

We do this first because so many authors leave it out, then wonder why their plot-driven book with static characters, no heartbeat, and lackluster emotion is not gripping readers.

If you've gotten this far and stayed present with the first ten lessons, you are well on your way to writing a great book.

Ignore what's confusing for now. We are in the middle of tuning a piano. There are still lots of variables that will slowly fall into place as you keep going.

So keep going! 20 more days left. Let's do this.

Day 11
A QUICK AND DIRTY PLOT

Today we make a slight shift in direction in terms of where we explore our novel next. We've spent the first ten days building out the underlying emotional skeleton of the book. Now, we'll build the muscles, organs, and flesh that will make our book function smoothly.

Eventually, we'll be using the five Tentpole Moments that are prevalent across most storytelling frameworks. You may have heard of them in some form or another before. These Tentpole Moments are:

- The Inciting Incident
- The Decision (aka the First Plot Point)
- The Reversal (aka the Midpoint)
- The "Cards on the Table" Moment (aka the Second Plot Point)

- The Transformation

I want to be clear that the Tentpole Moments are likely as old as the novel form itself. I didn't invent them or even observe them; they are simply the basis for storytelling architecture and their individual elements can be spotted in both modern novels and the classics.

As I said, we will be fleshing these out for your novel... eventually.

For now, though, we are going to do a quick and dirty version of the Tentpole Moments, using a portion of a little tool I invented (and still use to this day) called The Ultimate Novel Plotter.

Silly name, I know! But very effective in using what we already know (the character arc) and aligning it to our major plot points.

The Ultimate Novel Plotter starts with six questions that you answer for each character that has a character arc. They are:

- What is his or her fatal flaw?

- What is his or her difficult decision? (25% mark)

- What is his or her figurative death? (50% mark)

- How does the figurative death spring him or her into action? (How does he go from wanderer to warrior?)

- What is the final battle? (75% mark)
- What is the transformation?

We will go through each of these questions in a minute, but for now, I want to point out that you should already know the answer to the first and last questions! If not, now is your chance.

Here's how to find the answers to these questions quickly:

What is his or her fatal flaw? Learn about the fatal flaw in Day 7 - Character Fatal Flaws.

What is his or her difficult decision? (25% mark) The character has to choose between their ordinary world and their new quest or adventure. Ideally, neither of these choices is easy. Often, the protagonist is a reluctant hero!

What is his or her figurative death? (50% mark) The protagonist's life is either directly threatened or their fatal flaw is directly threatened (or both).

How does the figurative death spring him or her into action? (How does he go from wanderer to warrior?) For the first half of the book, the character is allowing things to happen to them. For the second half of the book, they will need to take action and make things happen themselves.

What is the final battle? (75% mark) There's one last piece of information that launches us into the end of the book. If you know what this piece of information is, and you know what the battle is, put that here!

What is the transformation? The character transforms because of the journey they've been on. What is the resolution to the story? Learn more about the transformation in Day 7 - Character Fatal Flaws.

Here are some examples of the answers to these six questions:

THE HARRY POTTER SERIES

Fatal Flaw: Harry Potter is afraid that he can't beat Voldemort; his fatal flaw is lack of confidence

Difficult Decision: Harry has to choose between what he knows (living with the Dursleys) and entering the strange and magical new wizarding world. In this particular series, the decision is not hard for him because life with the Dursleys is so horrible!

Figurative Death: Harry is playing quidditch and his life is literally threatened by someone in the stands (Hermione believes it to be Snape).

Wanderer to Warrior: Harry and his friends are determined to discover who is working with Voldemort as his ally to procure the philosopher's stone. Harry takes action by watching Snape's movements much more closely.

Final Battle: Harry and his friends learn that a mysterious person learned how to get past Hagrid's challenge. Fluffy guards the door to the philosopher's stone, and Hagrid has given away the secret. The trio (Harry, Ron, and Hermione) go after Voldemort's servant (whom they believe to be Snape) and enter the final challenges that lead to the end battle with Voldemort.

Transformation: Harry Potter recognizes his strengths where Voldemort is weak and uses those to his advantage to beat him.

THE HUNGER GAMES

Fatal Flaw: Katniss Everdeen doesn't want to bring children into this world because it's so terrible; her fatal flaw is she has no hope for the future.

Difficult Decision: She must choose between whether she is going to fight in the games so she can come home to her sister, mother, and Gale, or whether she is going to remain her surly, angry self in front of the cameras. Will she play the game that she morally opposes so deeply?

Figurative Death: Katniss nearly dies when she is forced to climb a tree to avoid battle with the Career Tributes. She gets stung by tracker jackers and begins hallucinating. Peeta, whom she believes is working against her, saves her life, which shifts her character arc, too. When he saves her, one of her false beliefs dies.

Wanderer to Warrior: Katniss teams up with Rue to take down some career tributes. Instead of avoiding the killings, she gets herself into the game and takes on a more active role. Her ideal outcome is to save Rue, who represents innocence and reminds us of Katniss's fatal flaw, her sister Primrose.

Final Battle: Katniss learns of the deaths of the last few tributes, specifically Thrash and Foxface. She reflects on what a part of her always knew, that the last battle will be at the Cornucopia with Cato. The last piece of information falls into place as well as Katniss scoops up the poisonous berries that took out Foxface and brings them with her to the final battle.

Transformation: Katniss learns that although there are terrible people and happenings in the world, specifically at the Capitol, there is plenty that is worth fighting for... including her new friend Peeta, and her safe return home.

THE FAULT IN OUR STARS

Fatal Flaw: Hazel wants her loved ones to move on unharmed after her death. She believes she is a grenade.

Difficult Decision: She decides not to fall in love with Augustus Waters, and to save him the pain when she dies. She does however start a friendship with him and they become obsessed with the ending to *An Imperial Affliction*.

Figurative Death: She kisses Augustus at Anne Frank's house tour in Amsterdam. They sleep together. She is completely all-in on their love, even though she still thinks of herself as a grenade.

Wanderer to Warrior: She learns that Augustus is going to die. Instead of backing away, she invests as much time as possible into his last days.

Final Battle: Augustus is gone and she's finished with his funeral. Peter van Houten, the author of *An Imperial Affliction*, tells her that Augustus was writing her something just before death. He might not have finished it. This is the last piece of information needed before Hazel goes into the final battle, which is confronting her own death with the people she loves.

Transformation: Hazel realizes that her death may hurt others, but she can still have a full life, even if it's a short one. She learns that her parents' lives will go on after her death. She learns that her mother will always be a mother. She tells Augustus that "some infinities are bigger than other infinities" and that she's happy for the small infinity he has given her (their romance).

PROMPTS

Question #1: What is your character's fatal flaw?

Learn about the fatal flaw in Day 7 - Character Fatal Flaws.

If you have multiple characters with character arcs, you'll need to answer this question for each character.

Question #2: What is his or her difficult decision?

The character has to choose between their ordinary world and their new quest or adventure.

Ideally, neither of these choices is easy.

Often, the protagonist is a reluctant hero (as in *The Hunger Games*), but sometimes (as in the *Harry Potter* series), the choice is more of a Cinderella moment.

This moment typically happens at the 25% mark of the book.

Question #3: What is his or her figurative death?

The protagonist's life is either directly threatened or their fatal flaw is directly threatened (or both).

This moment typically happens at the 50% mark of the book.

Question #4: How does the figurative death spring him or her into action?

For the first half of the book, the character is allowing things to happen to them.

For the second half of the book, they will need to take action and make things happen themselves.

How does he or she go from wanderer to warrior? What changes?

Question #5: What is the final battle?

There's one last piece of information that launches us into the end of the book. If you know what this piece of information is, and you know what the battle is, put that here!

This moment typically happens at the 75% mark of the book.

Question #6: What is the transformation?

The character transforms because of the journey they've been on. What is the resolution to the story? Learn more about the transformation in Day 7 - Character Fatal Flaws.

FEELING STUCK?

If you are feeling stuck on any of these questions aside from the first and last, there's no reason to fear as we'll be revisiting each one again over the coming days.

If you are feeling stuck on the questions about the fatal flaw and the transformation, head on back to Day 7 - Character Fatal Flaws.

Day 12

THE SETUP

Part 1, often called Act I or "The Setup" in other storytelling books, is roughly the first 10-25% of your story. It includes two important Tentpole Moments called the Inciting Incident and the Decision, which we'll get into later in this lesson. In general, it follows these rough beats:

- We introduce the reader to the protagonist's normal world, hopefully hooking them in the process

- Next, we explain to them why today is different for the protagonist. This is often the first clue leading up to the inciting incident—or it could even be the inciting incident.

- The inciting incident happens, and everything changes for the character. This is a surprising turn of fate type of moment. The inciting incident poses a question, and the protagonist will need to come up with an answer.

- Because of the inciting incident, the protagonist is faced with a decision. The decision is the answer to the question. That decision is the end of Part 1.

Every story opening follows this rough set of beats, no matter the genre. Let's do a few examples:

THE HARRY POTTER SERIES

Part 1 in *Harry Potter and the Sorcerer's/Philosopher's Stone* happens in the first few chapters. While the very first chapter (not from Harry's POV) sets the stage for the magic, Chapter 2 dives right into Harry in his ordinary world. Here, we learn about his ordinary life living in the space under the stairs, never getting anything his cousin Dudley has.

Next, he goes to the zoo and speaks to snakes accidentally—oops! Here's the "extraordinary day in the ordinary world" beat that clues us in that something in Harry's world is about the change.

Then, the inciting incident, when Harry receives his acceptance letter from Hogwarts (this is a long sequence that ends with Hagrid coming to collect him) presents Harry with a decision—become a part of the magical world and obey the rules, or stay with the Dursleys.

Finally, Harry makes his decision. It's an easy one

for him. He's headed to Hogwarts.

(Note: This takes him a few more chapters to fully decide he's going. When he gets on the train, he's finally reached the point of no return.)

THE HUNGER GAMES

Part 1 in The Hunger Games happens almost entirely in the first chapter. We meet Katniss in her ordinary world, a day of hunting in District 12. Then, we learn that today is an extraordinary day for her—it's Reaping Day. When her sister, Primrose's name is called (the inciting incident), Katniss is faced with her decision—let Prim go to the games or volunteer in her place.

(Note: Again, there are a few chapters of tearful goodbyes and whatnot before Katniss gets on the train, and reaches the true point of no return.)

THE MARTIAN

Part 1 in The Martian (the movie version) begins with an ordinary day on Mars, tending soil samples. Mark Watney is annoying his crew mates when a deadly storm comes rolling through (the extraordinary day within the ordinary world). The team makes an emergency departure, but Mark get hit with some debris and nearly dies. The crew can't find him, so they leave him and escape the storm (the inciting incident).

When Mark wakes up, he barely survives getting back to their bunker and has no way to contact NASA. He explains via a video diary that he has no food to survive for the four years it will take NASA to get to him. There are also a ton of other obstacles he faces. He's going to die on Mars.

He wallows for a bit, then finds a few potatoes that were sealed for a Thanksgiving celebration. Since he's a botanist, this is a potential solution to one of the obstacles he faces. He makes a decision—he's not going to die on Mars (the decision).

TENTPOLE MOMENT #1: THE INCITING INCIDENT

Let's discuss the inciting incident to clarify it, in case the examples aren't enough. The inciting incident is the thing that happens that forces your character to make a decision. It's the incident that shifts the story from passive to active. And it almost always pushes the protagonist to do something he or she wasn't expecting to have to do.

Additionally, the inciting incident can be one scene or a sequence of scenes, and it is usually foreshadowed by the contrast of "ordinary world" and "extraordinary day in ordinary world." The "extraordinary day" is often a hint at the inciting incident to come.

This beat is a Tentpole Moment in your story. You have to have it because it's the event that forces your character to make a decision, which pushes your story forward.

TENTPOLE MOMENT #2: THE DECISION (AKA THE FIRST PLOT POINT)

The Decision is another Tentpole Moment in your story. You have to have it because it launches the meat of your story. Without it, your story fizzles out and your character has no motivation to drive him forward.

It is often called the First Plot Point, but I'm not fond of that terminology because it doesn't provide any information for what this beat looks like. To me, the Decision is a major turning point for the character. They are presented with or forced into a situation. They do not get the choice to do nothing. There is no "hold on, let's think about that" option. They must pick. Now. And whatever they choose is usually life-changing, and dictates the rest of the story.

If you want to turn up the heat on the Decision, put your character in a no-win situation. For example, Katniss Everdeen in *The Hunger Games* is faced with two terrible choices:

- Let her sister go to the games and die
- Go to the games herself, even though she desperately doesn't want to be a "piece" in them—save her sister, but probably die herself

You don't have to do this, of course. Harry Potter,

DAY 12 : THE SETUP

for example, did not have a tough decision at all—or at least he didn't struggle with it, because the Dursleys are so terrible to him.

And in *The Martian*, Mark Watney's choice to survive isn't necessarily a hard choice either—at least not for an astronaut. Yes, there are people who would break down in the same situation, but it would be hard to believe a story where an astronaut breaks down, when they are specifically trained to do the opposite.

The Decision is also the end of Part 1 in this structure. It's the very last thing that happens. And once a character makes their decision, the path (and story) is launched. There's no turning back.

One thing I've noticed is that there's usually a lull after the decision is first made—a transition period before the character "really" hits the point of no return. To some extent, this gives the characters a chance for their decisions to truly sink in, or for them to continue their decision before they are truly forced to say "yes." In both *Harry Potter* and *The Hunger Games*, this point of no return is when the protagonist gets on the train.

I wouldn't personally get too specific about what the "true" First Plot Point is. Again, I'm not an academic; this just needs to help me write a great story. The easiest way to reconcile this is to realize that the Decision can last for multiple scenes, and it's nice to provide that longer transition from Part 1 to Part 2.

In *The Martian*, this lull happens differently, in the

sense that the decision is represented by Mark Watney's success at creating a greenhouse and growing the potatoes. If you want to get academic, you could say that section is already in Part 2, which is probably true for the novel (which I haven't read) but is sped up in the movie for length purposes.

Feel free to use your best judgment here and do what works best and makes the most sense for your story. Books are much more flexible than television or movies, so you can absolutely "eyeball" this and still get it right!

PROMPTS

Question #1: What is your protagonist's ordinary world?

Use the most basic information about your world and setting to ground your reader into your protagonist's reality. What does the average day look like for them?

Question #2: What is your protagonist's "extraordinary within the ordinary?"

For Harry Potter, he went to the zoo and spoke to snakes.

For Katniss Everdeen, it was Reaping Day, a once a year event where the Capitol drew names for tributes to the annual Hunger Games.

What's the "extraordinary within the ordinary" for your character(s)?

Question #3: What is the Inciting Incident?

Remember, the Inciting Incident poses a question, and the protagonist will need to come up with an answer.

If you're struggling with this, try phrasing the Decision (which we found in the Ultimate Novel Plotter lesson) as a question between the two choices. Then ask yourself, what scenario or incident forces my character to confront this decision?

Question #4: What is the Decision your character must make?

What are the two difficult choices (the rock and the hard place, ideally) that your character must choose between?

Question #5: What does your character decide, and how do you show that rather than tell it?

Harry leaves the Dursleys with a stranger just to escape them.

Katniss jumps into action, volunteering as tribute immediately after she hears her sister's name.

What scene can you create to show the reader the decision and the ultimate choice? And how can you amp it up to add more emotion?

FEELING STUCK?

In this lesson, we are revisiting some questions (and note that you are allowed to change your answers) and meeting a few other questions for the first time. There are still a few more opportunities to come where we will revisit these questions yet again, but as we near the midpoint of this 30-day novel prep, you should start to firm up your answers.

If the answers aren't coming, that's still okay. This 30-day period is set aside so you can prepare your novel and write it faster when you start drafting. If you aren't finding answers yet, you can still discover those answers while writing… and it may even be easier that way!

18 days to go.

Day 13
CHARACTERS IN THE ORPHAN ENERGY

The Hero Within: Six Archetypes We Live By by Carol Pearson describes story as four main archetypes or energies: Orphan Energy, Wanderer Energy, Warrior Energy, and Martyr Energy.

The Orphan Energy and The Setup correspond to the same portion of your novel, the first 25%. So while all of The Setup is happening in your plot, your characters are also energetically in a certain mindset.

The Orphan Energy is basically this: your characters are without a journey or quest. The quest will eventually "adopt" your character (through the inciting incident and the decision) and at that 25% mark, the energy for all of your main characters will shift.

Before this shift, you want to place anything that energetically matches the Orphan Energy into this first 25% "bucket" of your book. The Orphan Energy includes:

- Anything that already exists in your character's world that is well known to your character, such as transportation, politics, societal customs and values, situations, and more.

- Any established relationships with friends, family, enemies, mentors, or pets. Note that your character will probably be saying goodbye to most of these relationships once the quest adopts them.

- Any personality quirks or nicknames or scars that the character thinks nothing of, because he or she lives with it every day.

You can look through previous notes to fill out this section and also leave some space as the days go on to add to this section, as we explore other parts of your novel.

PROMPTS

Question #1: What worldbuilding belongs in the Orphan Energy and would be best introduced here?

The most important worldbuilding in this section will revolve around the protagonist's:

- Ordinary day

- Extraordinary within the ordinary event or happening

Think of all the worldbuilding pieces that they may encounter in their ordinary day.

Then, think of all the worldbuilding pieces that they may encounter in their extraordinary within the ordinary event.

Drop these in so that you can set the tone and mood of the book to begin with. It's always good to get some worldbuilding in early, as well, so you don't have an information dump later in the book.

Question #2: What relationships are best introduced during this section of the book?

Again, you want to think of why the protagonist would see in their ordinary day and extraordinary within the ordinary event.

I recommend mentioning family members, close friends, and anyone your character would see on a daily basis. This grounds the character in their regular world.

For these characters, note that you won't want to describe them in great detail. Limit yourself to a sentence max, if anything. Your character would not describe them in detail because they see them regularly!

The extraordinary within the ordinary event can highlight new characters, which you can describe in more detail.

For example, in *The Hunger Games*, Katniss describes Effie Trinket, Capitol visitor and Hunger Games Escort for District 12, in great detail, because she's out of the ordinary for District 12 and doesn't live there or visit often.

Question #3: What beliefs and worldviews does your protagonist have coming into this section of the book?

While it's ill advised to info dump in the first section of the book, you may want to include a little backstory on various characters and relationships they have with each other.

Note that you can also establish the backstories on these relationships by showing, not telling, so consider scenes that may work for this purpose!

You may also want to establish other beliefs through internal dialog or narrative summary. Not everything needs a scene.

Lastly, you'll want to come up with a decent way to introduce the fatal flaw of the book.

For example, in *New Moon*, the second book in *The Twilight Saga*, Bella Swan has a dream where she's an old woman standing next to the youthful looking, well-preserved, immortal vampire Edward.

This scene sets the stage for the entire book by showing the basic conflict in Bella and Edward's relationship. Bella doesn't want to grow old; Edward doesn't want to turn her into a vampire because she'll have to die and he wants to preserve her soul. This disagreement between them launches the main conflict of the book.

Question #4: What is your character's personality like at the beginning of the book?

How do they speak? What do they like? How do they spend their time?

What is their frustration with life? What are their goals and dreams (that are about to get interrupted)?

Question #5: Look at your beats so far for The Setup. How can you incorporate these notes into those beats as scenes and chapters?

Ideally, your notes from this section can pull double duty in scenes describing the ordinary world, "extraordinary within the ordinary," and so on.

FEELING STUCK?

The thing to remember about the Orphan Energy is that everything that matches this energy is in the protagonist's world before the book starts. It's all familiar and comfortable. Anything that feels uncomfortable to your character likely doesn't belong in the Orphan Energy. In the coming days, we will find the right spot for it!

17 more days to go.

Day 14

THE RESPONSE

Part 2, often called Act II or "The Response" in other storytelling books, is roughly the middle 11/25-50% of your story. It includes one Tentpole Moments that I call The Reversal (usually called the Midpoint). In general, this section follows this format:

- The character is pretty confused. He's trying to make his way in this "new reality" that he faces.

- He tries to take action, but he's still stumbling around. This means that most of his actions result in failures.

- He also often has the wrong goals. He may not be attacking his enemy directly, or he may be in survival or defense mode. It's not that he doesn't want to orient himself, he's just in a transition period where he doesn't have the right answers or solutions.

- There's often a mentor or some friends introduced in this section who help orient him toward his real goal.
- He may have to overcome his own beliefs and faults to orient himself properly.

All of this stumbling, false starting, and failure results in a pretty murky section where anything can go. This is where you as a writer begin to really start having power over how the story plays out. However, that also means it's easy to misstep and lose readers.

One way to make sure you don't misstep is to know exactly where you need to end up—at the Reversal, which is the end of Part 2.

TENTPOLE MOMENT #3: THE REVERSAL (AKA THE MIDPOINT)

The Reversal happens in the middle of the book and moves the character from this passive state of stumbling to an active state of doing and succeeding. It comes in two distinct flavors…

- The first is that something TOTALLY unexpected happens that threatens EVERYTHING the character knew and believed before. This is typically a critical piece of information that the protagonist doesn't have until now (even though sometimes, the reader can see it coming from a mile away). In *Star Wars*, this is when Vader tells Luke he is his father. In the classic Jane Austen novel *Emma*, this is when Emma finds out that Mr. Elton does not love Harriet—he loves Emma! This flavor of reversal needs to truly threaten the protagonist to the inner core, and on a deep emotional level. Here's your chance for the, "This changes everything" revelation.

- The second type of reversal is when a character looks death in the eye literally. In a thriller, there's no way out—the character thinks he's going to die. In an action/adventure, the character misses death by a hair or is rescued at the last minute. (It's sort of a dress rehearsal for the final battle.) In *Twilight*, Edward could have killed Bella but didn't, to both their surprises—and now she's irrevocably in love with him. (Seriously, it says that in the book.)

Let's do some examples:

THE HARRY POTTER SERIES

Part 2 in *Harry Potter and the Sorcerer's/Philosopher's Stone* happens right up to the midpoint of the book almost exactly.

He goes to school, makes friends, has some adventures, and gets into a bit of trouble with Snape. For the most part, he's a fish out of water, still feeling his way around the magical world and learning who to trust or not trust.

The Reversal happens when he realizes that the package Hagrid picked up is the philosopher's stone, and that's what's being safeguarded at the school. He believes Snape is after it, so he begins to actively stymy him in any attempts to obtain it!

He also faces a literal death during the quidditch game when someone in the stands (Hermione thinks it's Snape) tries to curse him while he's flying around on his broomstick.

THE HUNGER GAMES

Katniss Everdeen goes to the 74th annual Hunger Games but makes mistakes along the way. She rejects Peeta out of distrust, even though he cares deeply about her. She is a pawn in her team's plan to turn her into a silly girl for the cameras. She doesn't attack anyone or try to win once the games start (she's in survival mode). She's afraid of the Careers, especially, because she doesn't think she can beat them—and they are targeting her specifically due to her high scores in the pre-games.

Right in the middle of the book, when she gets stuck at the top of a tree with the Careers below her, she is confident she's going to die. There are five of them, one of her, and there's no way out.

But then, she sees Rue, who gives her a plan—to drop a nest of tracker jackers on the sleeping Careers below.

She does this and escapes death, with the help of Peeta. She learns two things:

- She is so certain she is going to die, but then she does not—this new piece of information means she could still win the games

- Peeta helped save her—is her distrust in him unfounded? Are all the things he's done up to that point (freezing her out, joining the careers, and so on) purposeful? Is he trying to help her survive?

Both of these are huge reversals, one for Katniss's external conflict and the other for her internal conflict.

You can see how both events would completely change her perspective on her situation. You can even see how she'd be going back through what she knows of Peeta, or the Careers, in her mind, seeing the past in a new light...

What's most interesting about this Reversal is that it's so symbolic. During this encounter, Katniss also gets her bow and arrows from Glitter, which moves her from prey (passive) to predator (active).

I wanted to point out this physical object (a symbol of her movement from Wanderer to Warrior) so you can see just how deeply aligned this Reversal is.

THE MARTIAN

Since *The Martian* is a survival story, the Reversal is both symbolic and external. Mark Watney accidentally blows a hole in the Hab, where his greenhouse is flourishing. This destroys his crop and all the supplies he used to create his crop, effectively cutting his food supply in half. He is staring death in the face at this point, because he can only survive about half the time he needs until the rescue mission can happen.

This is also a huge emotional blow. His greenhouse symbolized his first hope that he would survive Mars—that hope is now gone.

Whereas in *The Hunger Games* this twin journey is caused by two pieces falling into place, in The Martian the internal and external are the same.

TENTPOLE MOMENT #3: THE REVERSAL (AKA THE MIDPOINT)

The Reversal is another Tentpole Moment in your story. You have to have it because it moves your protagonist from passively fumbling around to actively attacking his or her enemies.

It is often called the Midpoint, but again I'm not fond of that terminology.

To me, the Reversal is a new and major piece of information that spurs the character into action. I already explained the two flavors of reversal, and as you might have already guessed, they are actually two sides of the same coin. One follows the external conflict. One follows the internal conflict.

The reversal can permeate in many ways that I think work well and mirror our own lives:

- When you reveal something new to the character that completely changes their perspective on everything. We'll discuss the idea of false beliefs in a later section, but it's when your character believes A but the truth is B. For example, a woman believes that her husband is trustworthy, then learns that he's been sleeping with her best friend, squandering all their money on tech gadgets, and lying about his past to everyone.

- When you shake the character out of their idiocy and watch them make real change. It's a point of complete frustration, where the character moves from sort-of-trying to I'm-going-to-figure-this-out-no-matter-what. In my own life, I had to "shake" myself out of sort-of-trying to be an author and get committed. This took a huge amount of change—I stopped accepting freelance work, I wrote faster and worked harder, I started releasing books every few months, I began networking with other authors even though I felt uncomfortable, and I even started putting more money into the effort. I had hit a breaking point and I was fed up with my failure.

- When your character hits "rock bottom" and thus has nothing to lose. He almost dies, but then he doesn't, so he starts to appreciate life more. Or all her efforts have made her situation worse, so she gives up and surrenders to her fate.

You can come up with your own Reversals, but hopefully this spurs some ideas.

The Reversal is also the end of Part 2 in this structure. Like the Decision, it can go on for several scenes or be made up of several pieces that all work together to cause change (as in *The Hunger Games*). The only rule is that it's big enough to move your protagonist from a passive state to an active state!

In *The Martian*, this Reversal is interesting, in that it does change the whole plan of waiting four years until the next mission lands. Now, the whole world (including the crew that left him behind) has to go on an active rescue mission in order for Mark Watney to survive.

In Part 2 of the story, most of the survival is due to Mark's actions.

In Part 3 of the story, it's NASA and his former crew that need to get active. This is something to keep in mind, especially when you have multiple protagonists or groups whose story arcs are going at once. You can piece this "passive to active" move together using multiple storylines!

PROMPTS

Question #1: What is the character's new reality?

What does the quest look like? Who is in control of the character or the character's environment? Who is the character dependent on?

Question #2: Who does the character trust and how do they make that decision?

Your protagonist will meet many new people during this phase. What situations help the trust (or show them to distrust) specific people?

What is their read on who is an ally or enemy?

Question #3: Which goals does the protagonist hit?

And which do they fail at?

Question #4: What is the antagonist force spotting?

During this part of the book, around the midpoint (37.5% or so through your novel), you want to have an encounter with the antagonistic force. This could be an attack from the villain or one of his henchmen, or it could be something simpler, like a reminder of why the couple can't be together, or a reminder of where the hero lacks confidence to succeed.

Question #5: What is The Reversal Moment?

Ideally, you match the external arc and the internal arc for a more impactful Reversal.

FEELING STUCK?

The Response section is, in my opinion, one of the most challenging sections of your novel to write because there's so much space to mess up!

Additionally, this section is quieter and doesn't have the big scenes that will show up in The Attack and The Resolution sections. That's because your characters are in Wanderer Energy, which we'll talk about in the next lesson.

If you're feeling a bit stuck on what challenges your protagonist should face in The Response, try starting with The Reversal scene and working your way backwards.

16 days left!

Day 15
CHARACTERS IN THE WANDERER ENERGY

The Wanderer Energy and The Response correspond to the same portion of your novel, the middle 25-50%. So while all of The Response is happening in your plot, your characters are also energetically in a certain mindset.

The Wanderer Energy is basically this: your characters are gathering resources and skills that will help them fight the antagonist. They are also following along with what others with more experience at this journey tell them to do.

I think of this energy as similar to a high school energy. At that age, you are sort of feeling like an adult in some ways. You are also still learning and growing and following the rules your parents and teachers have set for you.

All of this will shift at the midpoint of the book, when the energy moves from Wanderer to Warrior (passive to active).

Before this shift, you want to place anything that energetically matches the Wanderer Energy into this middle 25-50% "bucket" of your book. The Wanderer Energy includes:

- Any new transportation, politics, societal customs and values, weapons, beliefs, and more that your characters need to learn before facing the bad guy.

- Any new relationships with friends, family, enemies, mentors, or pets that your characters will need on the journey.

- Any mentor-to-mentee conversations that your characters need to have to understand what they are about to face.

- Any scheduling or training your character needs to face the bad guy at the end.

- Any new skills the character should acquire before moving into action. These can be acquired through challenges and false-belief breakthroughs too, of course!

This list is all about figuratively "heading back to school." In a young adult novel, the character is often going to a school of sorts. If the protagonist is not headed to school, they are headed to some sort of training, such as in *The Hunger Games* or *Divergent*.

In a mystery, the character may not have a school

or training facility to attend, but they are typically learning more about the case and following whatever clues they can. They often are fumbling blindly at this point and have no idea who they are really working for or who the bad guy is. They also have no idea who to trust, as someone will probably flip sides on them shortly!

You can look through previous notes to fill out this section and also leave some space as the days go on to add to this section, as we explore other parts of your novel.

PROMPTS

Question #1: What worldbuilding belongs in the Wanderer Energy and would be best introduced here?

This is a great place for new modes of transportation, exploring a new building or new world (as often there's transition travel as the energy of your novel shifts), or even throwing a party.

Question #2: What relationships are best introduced during this section of the book?

Ideally, your character meets new friends, new enemies, and new mentors at this point in the book.

Remember, they are also likely saying goodbye to old friends, mentors, and parents. We strip away their support system during the Orphan Energy and rebuild it during the Wanderer Energy.

Question #3: What beliefs and worldviews does your protagonist have coming into this section of the book?

Does your character need a backstory, an explanation, or an understanding of how things are currently done? This section is the place to put that.

Question #4: What training, skills acquisition, or mentoring needs to happen during this section of the book?

You can use experiences or sticky situations that the characters need to escape from, or you can do more formal skills acquisition through a school within the world, a weapons class, or some other teacher mentor relationship.

In a romance, this would look more like spending time together getting to know each other (or getting reacquainted). In a mystery, this would look more like finding or following clues.

Question #5: Look at your beats so far for The Response. How can you incorporate these notes into those beats as scenes and chapters?

Ideally, your notes from this section can pull double duty, specifically by incorporating them into the false beliefs breakthroughs that mark The Response section of your novel.

FEELING STUCK?

You've officially made it to the middle of the 30 days! Congrats!

If you feel stuck, make a list of everything the character needs to go on a big mission in The Attack part of the novel. This could be information, training, skills, objects, mentors, support, and so much more.

Now figure out, how is the character going to get all of these resources? Develop scenes around that.

15 more days to go.

Day 16

THE ATTACK

Part 3, often called Act II or "The Attack" in other storytelling books, is roughly the middle 50-75/90% of your story. It includes one Tentpole Moment that I call The "Cards on the Table" Moment.

In general, this section follows this format:

- The character has had his mind blown by the Reversal. It's enough to get him moving.

- The character actively goes after his main goal… and starts seeing success.

- He's actively moving closer to where he needs to be, entirely through his own actions and efforts.

- Things are sort of working. He's right more than he's wrong. He's almost ready to take on the antagonist.

- Your protagonist isn't a full-fledged hero yet, but he's learning and improving in Part 3. He is no longer stumbling and has moved firmly past his passive stage. Now that he's taking action, he accumulates information quickly and everything starts unfolding to the end of the story.

- The "Cards on the Table" Moment is the last piece of information the protagonist needs to go into the final battle. It is often called the Second Plot Point.

Let's do some examples:

THE HARRY POTTER SERIES

Once Harry Potter is convinced that Snape is trying to get the philosopher's stone for Voldemort, he springs into action and risks getting into trouble. He tracks Snape using his invisibility cloak. He actively tries to help Hagrid get rid of his illegal baby dragon, Norbert. He sneaks out to go after a teacher (he thinks it's Snape) and gets stuck in detention.

The "Cards on the Table" Moment comes when Harry learns that Hagrid has spilled the beans on how to get past Fluffy, the 3-headed creature that is the first line of defense against thieves, to a stranger who was clearly disguised.

At this point, Harry has all the information he needs. Voldemort knows everything he needs to know to retrieve the stone, and he'll be moving as quickly as possible via his helper, Snape (or so Harry thinks). So Harry recruits his friends to go in after Snape and get to the philosopher's stone first!

THE HUNGER GAMES

After the tracker jacker incident, Katniss teams up with Rue. They have their survival needs met for the moment (thanks to Katniss's new bow and arrow) and they make a plan to blow up the Careers' stash of food. They launch this attack and it's a success... but unfortunately, Rue dies in the process.

Then, the gamemakers change the rules and will now allow two winners if they are from the same district—which means she and Peeta could both survive and go home. She spends the next several chapters of the book rescuing him, keeping him alive, and even risking her own life to get him medicine.

During this whole section, she believes there's a chance she can win, and also bring Peeta home with her.

The "Cards on the Table" Moment starts when she delivers Peeta's medicine to him and he gets better—well enough for them to be a team in the games. He's not going to die due to his previous wounds; they can actually win this thing.

At this point, Katniss has all the information she needs. There are a few Tributes left, and if she and Peeta can beat them, they're going home.

Shortly after, resources come together and the last

few Tributes besides Cato are killed. Katniss also gets the last item she needs for battle: the poisonous berries. Neither she nor the reader knows how they will be used yet, but because they are the very last piece of information going into the last battle, this is how we know the "Cards on the Table" Moment is complete.

THE MARTIAN

In *The Martian*, Mark Watney has built his super-rover to get him to the Ares 4 landing site, where he will launch into space and rendezvous with his former crew members.

Likewise, the crew has picked up the supplies they needed and gotten all the way to Mars without a hitch.

And finally, the NASA team on the ground is doing everything they can to support the plan and are prepped on their end to get Mark through the terrible trials he must endure to get into space in the first place.

There may be some more "gotchas" in the final battle, but everything to succeed is in place. If they can pull this off, Mark gets to live.

DAY 16 : THE ATTACK

TENTPOLE MOMENT #4: THE "CARDS ON THE TABLE" MOMENT (AKA THE SECOND PLOT POINT)

I think of the "Cards on the Table" Moment as the trigger for the climax of the book. We are transitioning into Part 4 and we need to gear up and get ready.

The "Cards on the Table" Moment is at the end of Part 3 in this structure. It's another point of no return, similar to the Decision that ends Part 1. We're entering the final battle, where the character will succeed or fail. Everything is in place for him to succeed—but the final battle is where we find out if he will succeed. No new information can enter the story for the finale, unless it was seeded in the first three parts!

PROMPTS

Question #1: What is the first action your protagonist takes after The Reversal?

How does the protagonist feel?

What do they need to digest after this big moment? How does it affect their worldview moving forward?

Make sure the answer to this puts your character in motion! Action is critical at this point, even if it's not the right action for your character to take.

Question #2: Where and how does your protagonist test his or her skills in the real world?

The challenges are getting harder in this section, and ideally the protagonist is using skills learned in the last section in the actual world by this point.

What is the most challenging situation you can put them in, that will stretch their abilities to the max?

And how can you build on their current skills and throw them a curve ball or two?

Question #3: What are the resources, skills, and objects your protagonist needs for the final battle?

Now that he's taking action, he accumulates information quickly and everything starts unfolding to the end of the story.

What is the natural progression of testing your character's skills and abilities and collecting resources for the final battle?

Question #4: What is the antagonist force spotting?

During this part of the book, around the midpoint (62.5% or so through your novel), you want to have another encounter with the antagonistic force. This could be an attack from the villain or one of his henchmen, or it could be something simpler, like a reminder of why the couple can't be together, or a reminder of where the hero lacks confidence to succeed.

Question #5: What is the "Cards on the Table" Moment?

This moment is the last piece of information the protagonist needs to go into the final battle. What is it for your character?

Make a list of everything they will need in the final battle, including a few things that could come in handy or be a helpful surprise.

It sometimes helps to work backward, here!

FEELING STUCK?

When searching for the "Cards on the Table" Moment, I always look at the final battle sequence. It goes like this:

- The hero and the villain fight

- The hero gets the best of the villain temporarily due to cleverness that hits the villain at his fatal flaw

- Then, the villain strikes back and gets the best of the hero temporarily due to cleverness that hits the hero at his fatal flaw

- The hero then needs one last (smart and clever) thing in his back pocket, that helps him barely win

- What is that last-ditch effort in his back pocket during that battle scene?

That makes a great basis for the "Cards on the Table" Moment. Start there!

(Of course, you can use anything else from the first 75% of your book too. There are no hard and fast rules; this is just an idea for getting unstuck.)

14 days left!

Day 17
CHARACTERS IN THE WARRIOR ENERGY

The Warrior Energy and The Attack correspond to the same portion of your novel, the middle 50-75%. So while all of The Attack is happening in your plot, your characters are also energetically in a certain mindset.

The Warrior Energy is basically this: your characters are all in and determined to take control of the situation after The Reversal. They may be frustrated, angry, or disappointed and want blood, revenge, or to win against the antagonist.

All of this will shift leading up to the final battle or climax of the book, when the energy moves from Warrior to Martyr.

Before this shift, you want to place anything that energetically matches the Warrior Energy into this middle 50-75% "bucket" of your book. The Warrior Energy includes:

- Starting fights rather than just responding to them
- Adventures, missions, attacks, and more
- Solving puzzles and clues and circling in on the antagonist
- Actively pursuing relationships, or committing to relationships in a new way
- It can also still include new weapons, transportation, mentee conversations, and more, but your character should be out of high school energy and "graduated" to the real world, so they should encounter these in situations and ideally having some experience with a similar weapon or transportation

You can look through previous notes to fill out this section and also leave some space as the days go on to add to this section, as we explore other parts of your novel.

PROMPTS

Question #1: What worldbuilding belongs in the Warrior Energy and would be best introduced here?

This is still a great place for new modes of transportation, exploring a new building or new world, or even throwing a party.

You can also introduce new mentors, weapons, relationships, or challenges, as long as they build off of knowledge obtained in the Wanderer Energy.

Question #2: How do relationships forged in the Wanderer Energy portion of the book grow?

This is a great time to build or solidify long-term relationships between friends or lovers. It's also often a time when the protagonist begins to break free of the mentor or mentors. They will eventually have to face the enemy alone.

Question #3: What beliefs and worldviews does your protagonist have coming into this section of the book?

Does your character need a backstory, an explanation, or an understanding of how things are currently done? This section is the place to put that.

Question #4: What challenges can build off of the training acquired in the last section?

Take everything you've been training the character for and put it to use in the field! Keep in mind that training can't fully prepare you for real dangers you encounter in the real world.

If you're writing a romance, this is where you test the relationship. If you're writing a mystery, this is where you test the character's problem-solving chops!

Give them something savage to deal with here!

Question #5: Look at your beats so far for The Attack. How can you incorporate these notes into those beats as scenes and chapters?

Ideally, your notes from this section can pull double duty, specifically by incorporating them into the false beliefs breakthroughs that mark The Attack section of your novel.

FEELING STUCK?

If you are feeling stuck, I highly recommend coming up with a dangerous mission or adventure for the protagonist to go on.

If that fails, look at The Response and see what you have to bring forward. You can also look at The Resolution and think through what needs to happen before the protagonist heads into the final battle and work backwards.

13 days to the end—you're almost there!

Day 18
THE RESOLUTION

Part 4, often called Act III or "The Resolution" in other storytelling books, is roughly the last 75-100% of your story. It includes one Tentpole Moment that I call The Transformation. In general, this section follows this format:

- The character has everything he needs after the "Cards on the Table" Moment. No new information can be introduced. That doesn't mean there won't be a twist, it just needs to have been seeded and foreshadowed in the previous 3/4ths of the book.
- The character is entering the final battle, which has several ups and downs, including a moment where he comes very close to losing.
- Just as he's about to lose, something clicks into

place and he sees another opportunity or way to escape.

- He escapes and goes after the antagonist again, this time winning the battle.

- There's usually several pages of resolution that come afterward to wrap up any loose ends in the story.

Your protagonist has earned the right to be a called a hero in Part 4. This means that he is the one who ultimately saved the day (not his friends—though they are allowed to help him), and that there was no deus ex machina going on (when something happens by chance that allows the protagonist to win).

THE HARRY POTTER SERIES

Harry can't get any of the adults to listen to him, so he and his friends go after Voldemort themselves. They face obstacles that all of the professors have set for them, each one unique to that professor's special skill sets.

The three of them continue through most of the obstacles, but eventually Harry is forced to go on alone as his friends get "taken out" (they're safe, of course). This means that Harry gets to be the sole hero who faces down Voldemort's ally—who ends up being another teacher, Quirrell, rather than Snape.

He is able to stop Quirrell thanks mostly to several pieces that were already in play. Quirrell/Voldemort can't touch him due to the spell cast on him as a child, and he has already learned how to use the mirror of the erised by chance earlier in the book, which is how he finds the philosopher's stone in his pocket.

He defeats Quirrell but ends up in the infirmary, and his first year at Hogwarts (and the story) winds down after he makes a full recovery.

THE HUNGER GAMES

Katniss and Peeta are forced toward the Cornucopia to face the last Tribute in their way—Cato. But they are ambushed by mutts that represent the deaths of each of the Tributes. These mutts chase them up the Cornucopia, where they face off with Cato. They figure out a way to kill him and wait for hours before he dies, so the games can be over.

There's a twist in the final battle, as Katniss and Peeta do not automatically win—the rules change again, and only one of them can do so now. Katniss is not willing to accept that. She forces the Capitol to declare them both winners by threatening to poison both of them with the berries they found earlier.

The Capitol is not happy about that and they almost don't make it back home, but Katniss manages to convince them that it wasn't an act of defiance, it was only because she was so desperately in love with Peeta and couldn't bear to part from him (a Romeo and Juliet moment).

They do make it home—but now Katniss has a target on her back. Get ready for Book 2!

THE MARTIAN

Mark gets ready on the ground for liftoff, and NASA projects him into the air—though his acceleration is off target.

His crew makes sacrifices on their end to get closer to him—but they are still pretty far apart, too far for a normal interception.

The commander of the mission goes as far out into space as she can to catch Mark Watney—but he's still too far away.

Mark then pokes a hole in his suit and uses the escaping air to steer himself closer to her, saving himself (with a lot of help from the rest of the world, of course).

TENTPOLE MOMENT #5: THE TRANSFORMATION

The Transformation is the last Tentpole Moment in the story. The protagonist must have an internal change to go with the external change that allowed him or her to win the final battle.

- For Harry, the internal change was that he got past his vision of his parents in mirror of the erised. He no longer desired to be with them, without his scar, and that's why he was able to see the philosopher's stone in his pocket. Letting go of his parents is an important part of his larger character arc.

- For Katniss, the internal change was that she stood up to the Capitol, her real enemy. Up until this point, she had been too scared to fight back against them. She saw the other Tributes as her enemies, even though all of them are the victims.

- For Mark, the internal change was really just that he actually survived. Although he wasn't ever going to give up trying to survive, he probably didn't truly believe he would survive until he reached Ares 3 and was finally safe.

The Transformation is an important part of the climax of the story, and is a big factor in the overall emotional impact you make on your reader!

PROMPTS

Question #1: Where, when, and how do the hero and villain meet for the final battle?

What brings them to confrontation? Who else is there?

Question #2: How does the hero get the best of the villain?

The hero gets the best of the villain temporarily

due to cleverness that hits the villain at his fatal flaw.

What is the villain's fatal flaw? How is that your hero's greatest strength?

Question #3: How does the villain get the best of the hero?

Then, the villain strikes back and gets the best of the hero temporarily due to cleverness that hits the hero at his fatal flaw.

What will hit the hero the hardest, based on his fatal flaw? Get to the heart of what the villain could do to the hero to destroy him!

Remember, the hero could lose everything in this battle. In most cases, he's literally risking his life.

Question #4: What is the thing in the hero's back pocket that ultimately leads to his victory?

The hero then needs one last (smart and clever) thing in his back pocket, that helps him barely win.

What is it? When did the reader first encounter it?

Question #5: What else needs to be resolved?

What conversations need to be had?

What open loops need to close (and which do you intend to leave open to entice the reader to Book 2)?

What else needs to be explained to the reader? Specifically, how does the reader know the villain's side of the story?

DAY 18 : THE RESOLUTION

FEELING STUCK?

The Resolution is very straightforward if you just follow the beats of the battle. If you're feeling stuck, go back to the fatal flaws for the hero and the villain.

You can also give the final battle a unique visual setting that provides additional excitement. For example, in the movie *Breaking Dawn: Part 2* from the *Twilight Saga*, they place the final battle in a huge, snow white open field in the dead of winter. There is no cover from trees, and the two sides are completely exposed—everyone can see everyone else coming from a mile away.

12 days to go!

Day 19
CHARACTERS IN THE MARTYR ENERGY

The Martyr Energy and The Resolution correspond to the same portion of your novel, the end 75-100%. So while all of The Resolution is happening in your plot, your characters are also energetically in a certain mindset.

The Martyr Energy is basically this: your characters is sacrificing himself or herself to save the world, the relationship, the team, his or her own life, or whatever else is at stake.

There's a possibility of death (or if you're writing a romance, of heartbreak), but ideally the characters succeed. They may (and probably will) have to sacrifice a part of themselves for the greater good.

The Martyr Energy is a chance to wrap up any loose threads that you've left through your novel.

These can be of the odd nature.

For example, if someone lost a weapon at the midpoint, you may need to recover it before the end. A great example of this is Gryffindor's Sword from the *Harry Potter* series, which disappears in the middle of Book 7 and appears at the end when needed.

Another example might be a phrase that appears at the beginning of the story. A great example of this is in the movie, *He's Just Not That Into You*, where Gigi states at the beginning that, "We have to stop listening to these stories" because they are "the exception, not the rule." When the love interest comes back around at the end, she declares, "I'm the exception."

There are a lot of threads to tie up, so think through as much as you can now and make a note to close those loops where needed.

PROMPTS

Question #1: What worldbuilding objects or elements might need to be wrapped up before the end of the book?

Consider things like transportation, buildings, laws, politics, magic, weapons, and more.

Question #2: What relationships need to be resolved before the end of the book?

It's especially important to wrap up or provide resolution for the protagonist's relationships. Remember, they have changed throughout the book, so it's likely that their key relationships have shifted too.

Question #3: What clever ways can you bring something from the beginning of the book to the end?

A simple phrase, symbol, or motif can work very well here, and is often done to represent the fatal flaw or theme. For example, in the movie *The Martian*, they used a single green sprout to represent Mark Watney's hope of survival.

Question #4: Look at your beats so far for The Resolution. How can you incorporate these notes into those beats as scenes and chapters?

Ideally, your notes from this section can pull double duty, specifically by incorporating them into the final battle of your novel.

FEELING STUCK?

You've reached the end of a long section that follows the traditional 4-part storytelling structure.

I hope you have gained a lot from these 9 days of focus in this area!

If you are struggling with any of these questions, we'll be revisiting many of them again before we end the 30 days, so hang tight.

Either way, you've made a ton of progress on

DAY 19 : MARTYR ENERGY

prepping your novel!
11 days to go. Let's shift gears again...

Day 20
THEMATIC ELEMENTS: GROUP AND CHARACTER SYMBOLISM

Once you have your character and plot arcs laid out and matching the concept and theme, you can reinforce everything with thematic elements.

What is a thematic element? It's a representation of an idea in a different format.

For example, Harry Potter's fatal flaw is his lack of confidence in living up to his "Chosen One" status when everyone is counting on him to bring down Voldemort.

How is it represented? As a scar across his forehead, for everyone to see. Even those who don't know him personally can take one look at his face and find the famous lightning bolt that made him "The Boy Who Lived."

The scar is a thematic element. It's a representation of Harry Potter's fatal flaw.

Thematic elements are critical, purposeful, and

found in every breakout hit series.

Katniss Everdeen of *The Hunger Games* has a mockingjay pin that eventually represents her role in the war as she literally becomes the mockingjay.

Bella Swan of the *Twilight Saga* has her clumsiness, a constant reminder of her fragility as a human and the danger that looms over them if Edward doesn't turn her into a vampire. She later receives a crescent-shaped scar where Edward has literally sucked poison that could change her into a vampire from her body—another representation of his hope for her soul and his ability to not kill her.

Here's a list of potential items that can serve as thematic elements in your story:

- Mood
- Objects (Jewelry, Weapons, Creatures)
- Motifs
- Metaphors
- Quotes
- Symbols
- Anecdotes
- Phrases
- Iconography
- New Vocabulary
- Character Quirks

- Metaphors
- Repeated patterns (visual or written)
- "Painting the picture" (emotional and mood words)
- Names
- Locations, Places, Settings
- Weather

Today, we're focused on how we can give thematic elements to your characters, groups, and character arcs. The best way to see how to do this is through example, so let's dive in to several!

FATAL FLAW AND MOTIVATION TO THEMATIC ELEMENTS

If you aren't sure where to start coming up with thematic elements, look to your fatal flaw and character motivation. These are prime opportunities to create symbolic meaning through objects or artifacts within your world. Here are some examples:

The Protagonist's Shorthand

On *Revenge*, Emily Thorne draws a symbol that represents her quest for revenge, Infinity x Infinity. We learn that she got this from her father and it was originally a way for them to tell each other they

DAY 20 : THEMATIC ELEMENTS

loved each other. That symbol has been repurposed for Emily's revenge mission and comes up over and over again as a recurring motif throughout the series.

It doesn't just symbolize her revenge plot though. It's also used to remind viewers that in the midst of all the terrible Emily Thorne-y things she's doing, the young and ruined Amanda Clarke is still in there. She's still a good guy, she's still justified in her actions, and therefore we can still root for her, despite her desire to get revenge, which is usually a rather ugly trait in someone.

Infinity x Infinity eventually becomes Emily's tell. It's a symbol that only Victoria is capable of matching to the young Amanda Clarke—and poetically, Emily's fatal flaw becomes her nemesis's weapon.

The Antagonist's Fatal Flaw and Motivation

In the *Hunger Games* trilogy, the Capitol is in trouble. Their fatal flaw is that by using the games, they've accidentally sparked a rebellion. This is represented by the mockingjay, which is also an accidental creation of theirs from mixing animal DNA to form new mutations.

The mockingjay starts as Katniss's lapel pin. It grows into a full-fledged suit that Katniss wears as she becomes the Mockingjay (starting when she shoots her arrow into the force field in Book 2).

This symbol soon becomes the symbol for the rebellion, transcending Katniss herself and representing something more.

GOAL AND FALSE BELIEFS TO THEMATIC ELEMENTS

Your tentpole moments (usually represented as a goal/false belief combo) are also a fantastic place to look for opportunities for symbolism. Here are some examples:

The Hunger Games Bow and Arrow

In *The Hunger Games*, Katniss knows that she can only win the games if she finds the bow and arrow from the Cornucopia. She isn't able to retrieve it during the first few minutes of the games, and rival Glitter grabs it instead so she must wait.

But she does eventually reclaim the bow and arrow during the Reversal moment, which is also when she transitions from passive to active (from Wanderer to Warrior). Before she has the bow and arrow, she's only trying to survive. After she gets her bow and arrow, she begins hunting her opponents and actively trying to win the games.

This is small and subtle, but incredibly clever on author Suzanne Collins part!

DAY 20 : THEMATIC ELEMENTS

PROMPTS

Question #1: Look at the list of potential thematic elements. Can you come up with an example related to groups, characters, and character arcs for each option I listed?

For example, George R.R. Martin has littered his *A Song of Ice and Fire* world with thematic elements, giving emblems and catchphrases to each of the family houses and some of the individual characters too.

You could say that stuff like "a Lannister always pays his debts" is a thematic element specifically for Tyrion Lannister, also known as the imp. It reminds the reader (or viewer) that Tyrion might be small and unable to fight like his older brother Jamie, but always uses money and his father's name to survive a difficult situation.

Do any of these examples you've come up with spark ideas for your own novel?

Question #2: How can you create a thematic element for your character's fatal flaw?

Don't feel weird about reusing popular ideas, like a scar, a tattoo, a piece of jewelry, a special weapon, a phrase, or anything else. Readers love it!

Question #3: How can you map different thematic elements onto your Tentpole Moments?

For example, you could symbolize The Decision by two objects representing two choices, or symbolize the transition from Wanderer to Warrior with a weapon, or symbolize the final battle by having the hero save his work partner and his romantic partner at the same time. There are lots of possibilities here!

FEELING STUCK?

The best way to come up with thematic elements is to start paying attention to all the fiction you read and watch.

Yes—that Netflix time is actually productive! Who would have thought?

Look at how television, movies, and books use thematic elements as shorthand for the reader, to remind them of a concept or just tickle their enjoyment of the story.

Try to take each one you notice and ask, "Is there a way I could do something like this in my novel?"

Not all will work, but some will.

10 days to go!

Day 21
THEMATIC ELEMENTS: THEME, SETTING, AND WORLDBUILDING

Today, we are continuing our look at thematic elements in your novel. For your convenience, here is the list of potential thematic elements again:

- Mood
- Objects (Jewelry, Weapons, Creatures)
- Motifs
- Metaphors
- Quotes
- Symbols
- Anecdotes
- Phrases
- Iconography

- New Vocabulary
- Character Quirks
- Metaphors
- Repeated patterns (visual or written)
- "Painting the picture" (emotional and mood words)
- Names
- Locations, Places, Settings
- Weather

Let's do some examples for how this gets embedded into the theme, setting, and worldbuilding.

THEME AND WORLDBUILDING TO THEMATIC ELEMENTS

A Fault In Our Stars and the Reversal

When Hazel and Augustus from *The Fault in Our Stars* finally kiss, it's on a tour of Anne Frank's house. Anne Frank is a young woman who lived a short but good and impactful life, which matches Hazel's acceptance that her life will be short but can be good, and that it's worth it to have loved and lost, as the two of them are fated to do. When she learns about Augustus's cancer, it only reinforces the moment, because their time is even shorter than she realized, and she is the one who will have to survive and live with the "scars" he gifts her from their love.

The Fault in Our Stars happens to be heavy on the metaphors, quotables, anecdotes, and symbolic representations of the theme at every turn, so I won't list them all here—but if you have the chance, grab the book and read or reread it. It's a quick one, and you'll be surprised at how much of this framework applies to that novel. (And don't forget, it was a breakout novel!)

Gone Girl and Anniversary Presents

In the movie *Gone Girl*, we learn at the Reversal moment that Amy is still alive and well. At the same time, her husband Nick solves her last clue of their anniversary scavenger hunt, revealing the marriage present that she's left him—framing him for her murder. Everything about this reveal, from the symbolic anniversary scavenger hunt, to where she leaves the present, represents the real theme of the story—a marriage with so much pain and hurt that one member enacts revenge on the other.

Names and Locations to Thematic Elements

We haven't talked much about names and locations, so I wanted to bring them up here. Your character names, location names, and even your book title are fantastic places to hint at theme! Here are a few examples:

- J.K. Rowling is the master of naming things and comes up with some fun ones, including Kreacher (the house elf), Diagon Alley and Knockturn Alley (the darker marketplace), Flourish and Blotts (an ink and paper store), Tom Riddle, and more.

- *The Fault in Our Stars* is a reference to a Shakespearan quote, "The fault, dear Brutus is not in our stars, But in ourselves." Author John Green explained that he does not agree with this quote, and sometimes bad things do happen that are out of our control.

- The names *Twilight*, *New Moon*, and *Eclipse* are all references to how the moon relates to Bella and Edward's relationship in the book.

- Emily Thorne is a thorn in Victoria Grayson's side; she sends black thorny roses to Victoria to inflict emotional pain on her.

- Although *A Song of Ice and Fire* has not yet been completed at the time of this writing, most fans (including myself) suspect that the final battle will be between the White Walkers (ice) and Dragons (fire).

PROMPTS

Question #1: Look at the list of potential thematic elements. Can you come up with an example related to theme, setting, or worldbuilding for each option I listed?

Do any of these examples you've come up with spark ideas for your own novel?

Question #2: How can you build thematic elements into names and locations?

If you feel stuck on this, check out what JK Rowling does, as she is the queen of creating names.

Question #3: How can you build thematic elements into the theme itself, to remind your reader of the point of the book?

Think through what your story or characters might be a metaphor for, then look for actual metaphors that you can layer into your book (such as Anne Frank's house tour in *The Fault in Our Stars*).

Be wary of getting too heavy-handed, however, unless that's what you are going for.

FEELING STUCK?

Thematic elements are meant to be fun and to add deeper meaning and subtext to your story. Don't feel like you have to come up with everything at once. You intuitively know how to add thematic elements to your story already and may even be doing it without realizing it.

Let yourself stay open to the possibilities for symbolism and let the right ideas flow as you continue to prepare your novel.

9 days left!

Day 22
SETTING AND WORLD: PLACE

We're shifting gears again, this time to worldbuilding.

Even if you are not writing fantasy or science fiction, you still must build your world!

In the last few lessons on thematic elements, I gave you several examples including *Revenge* and *Gone Girl* where worldbuilding became important, even though those stories were set in a modern, present-day, non-magical world.

For the next three days, we're going to explore the landscape and backdrop of your novel. All you have to do is answer a few questions about what you know about your world so far.

PROMPTS

Question #1: What is the geography of your world like?

If it's set in modern day, what is the setting? What city? What is the weather like? Does it match the mood of the book and characters?

If it's set in a fantasy world or in the past of future, what are the surrounding cities like? How does your place (country, city, however you want to define it) feel in relationship to others around it?

Question #2: What are the different "sets" for your story?

Where do your characters travel to (if anywhere)? How do they get between places?

What is the personality of each place? How do these places contrast each other?

Do specific characters feel more in their comfort zone in different places? Do specific characters better match one place over another (and what does this mean for their character and for the larger story)?

FEELING STUCK?

I'm not a huge fan of doing a ton of worldbuilding for your book ahead of time because it's very easy to get lost in it and never move forward with your story. I genuinely believe the most important parts of your

DAY 22 : SETTING AND WORLD

world will come to you while writing, and that this is the most efficient way to get started. Don't worry too much if you are unsure of the answers to any of these questions. The right places will emerge when needed!

8 more days...

Day 23
SETTING AND WORLD: LIFE AND CULTURE

Today we're continuing with worldbuilding and focusing on life and culture.

Even if your book is set in a non-magical modern day place, you're likely painting a surreal version of that place to heighten the interest in your story and create a bit more drama.

For example, the book and show *Big Little Lies* is set in Monterey, California in the present day. But the author Liane Moriarty paints a glitzy lifestyle of big mansions, overbearing moms to 6-year olds, and crazy personal drama that spills over into a murder mystery.

This isn't just modern-day, it's an over-the-top representation of a small, tight-knit community.

Here are some of the things you might want to consider about the life and culture in your world:

DAY 23: SETTING AND WORLD

- Languages
- Ethnicities
- Religion
- Food and Drink
- Entertainment
- Societal Classes

PROMPTS

Question #1: What are the different social classes?

How do they rank in relation to one another? Where do each of your characters fit in?

What does the disparity between classes mean for your world and for each of your characters?

Question #2: What identity-based labels drive your characters?

Ethnicity and religion are bound to have a huge impact on each of your characters. How do these identity-based labels change who they are? Remember, these are just large Groups and can be treated as such in your novel.

Question #3: What do people do for fun in your world?

What do they eat and drink? How do they survive? What is work like? What is home life like? What do they do for entertainment?

Remember, much of this will be based on the rest of the cultural decisions you've already made for your character. You may need to show disparity across each of these categories to further emphasize class, ethnicity, and religion.

FEELING STUCK?

For me, worldbuilding is sometimes more easily inspired through pictures. Have a look at some images online (use a stock photo site, grab some magazines and scissors, or check out DeviantArt for a variety of imagery) and try to create a vision board of what your world looks like. Take it a step further and find people who look and dress like how you'd imagine they would in your world.

Do the visuals help you flesh this out in words?

7 days (one week!) left to go… are you feeling good about your novel yet?

Day 24
SETTING AND WORLD: HISTORY, TECHNOLOGY, AND LAW

Today we are wrapping up our short foray into worldbuilding with a focus on how society runs.

Here are some of the things you might want to consider about the history, technology, and law in your world:

- How the government runs/works
- Any magical systems needed
- The historical way of doing things and what influenced that
- Political systems, climate, issues
- Wars
- Weapons
- Transportation

- Digital devices

It's my experience that this level of worldbuilding can lead you down a rabbit hole, so don't go overboard just yet! Think through each of these pieces, but only to the extent that it is relevant to your characters and plot.

PROMPTS

Question #1: What systems are important to your story?

If your characters interact with the government or another large organization (a school, a church, a magical community, a military, and so on) it's important to understand exactly how the system works. What are the rules your character will need to know to survive in these communities?

Question #2: What wars and other historical events or markers are important to your story?

Worldviews are shaped by historical events that happen before and during a person's lifetime. What has your character experienced?

Wars in particular shape worldviews, law, society, and other policies and regulations that we all live by.

Question #3: What weapons, transportation, and other technology are important to your story?

Keep in mind that weapons, transportation, and technology play a huge role in war. Make sure all of this is aligned!

FEELING STUCK?

If you want to dive deeper into worldbuilding, you may enjoy exploring other books on the topic. My favorite is *Storyworld First: Creating a Unique Fantasy World for Your Novel* by Jill Williamson.

But with only 6 days left, I would hold off on doing any more worldbuilding for now, as we're nearing the end of the 30 days. Get excited!

Day 25

THE TREATMENT

We are headed into the home stretch of our novel writing prep! Congratulations for making it this far. Most people don't, so seriously—give yourself some real kudos for getting to Day 25!

For the next five days, we will be finishing up with the rest of my tool, The Ultimate Novel Plotter. If you recall, we first discussed this tool on Day 11 - A Quick and Dirty Plot. As I mentioned before, this is set of worksheets that I use to quickly plot a book in less than a day.

Throughout the past 30 days, you've learned all the concepts you need to know to fill out this set of worksheets. We've taken each little piece step-by-step and broken it all down so you can learn the concepts and apply them correctly. We've visited and revisited the most important prompts so you can take a few shots at them and grow your story organically.

DAY 25 : THE TREATMENT

Now, we're going to revisit everything one last time and see if we can organize it all into a cohesive story.

The last six days of this novel prep plan have no prompts. Instead, we are going to take the things we've already discovered about our novel and order them appropriately.

This is your last chance to visit the questions we've uncovered through this book. If you want to come up with an answer to each, now is the time!

If not, that's also perfectly fine. You will have yet another chance to discover these answers (or change them) as you are writing.

Open a new document, create a new board or mind map, or do whatever else needed to start with a blank space.

Additionally, have your notes on your novel from the past 24 days at the ready. You'll be referencing them quite a bit!

Lastly, the reason we're starting with a blank space is so you can feel free to revise and make decisions as you go back through your notes. You've now had time and lots of prompts to think through various aspects of your novel. Use the blank space to "revise" your novel before you even write it!

Think about it... why write a bunch of scenes you're not even going to use in the end?

Don't be afraid to make a change now, as it will be make everything down the line much easier.

ULTIMATE NOVEL PLOTTER: THE TREATMENT

Use this template as a guide for completing the first section of the Ultimate Novel Plotter: The Treatment.

- What is the novel about? Refer back to the concept and theme.
- Who are the key characters in the novel?
    - What are their storylines? Their transformation journeys?
    - How and when are they introduced in the book (choose between The Setup, The Response, The Attack, The Resolution)?
    - What are their key group affiliations? How do these change throughout the book?
    - What are their key relationships? How do these change throughout the book?
    - What are their key thematic elements? When are these introduced throughout the book (choose between The Setup, The Response, The Attack, The Resolution)?
    - What is the fatal flaw and motivation?
    - What are the false beliefs and goals?

DAY 25 : THE TREATMENT

- Where and when does the story take place?
  - What are the key locations?
  - What are the key aspects of the world? How and when are they introduced in the book (choose between The Setup, The Response, The Attack, The Resolution)?

Press On, Igniter!

Day 26

OUTLINING 0-25%

Next, you are going to map out the rough beats for the first 25% of the novel.

THE FAULT IN OUR STARS

> **Part 1:** August and Hazel are just getting to know one another. There is a lot of flirting back and forth, but it's slow-going because Hazel does not want to get too close.
> **Inciting Incident:** Hazel and Augustus have a disagreement at support group on the topic of oblivion. They are far apart on the issue. This is a genre tentpole moment in romance novels, where the hero and heroine meet.
> **The Decision:** One night, Hazel and Augustus stay up talking on the phone until all hours of the night. Although she has tried to keep

him at bay, she is in too deep. They've even picked out their couple flirting device, which is "Okay." This is the point of no return. Hazel and Augustus also decide they will have an ending to *An Imperial Affliction*, which launches their external journey.

ULTIMATE NOVEL PLOTTER: THE SETUP (FIRST 25% OF YOUR NOVEL)

Use this template as a guide for completing the second section of the Ultimate Novel Plotter: The Setup. I've included my questions plus some simple notes that may or may not help you refine your answers.

- What is the protagonist's normal world?
    - Have a great and surprising opening line that demonstrates tension or two opposing forces
    - Focus on three words that you want people to use to describe your reader—then develop a scene that demonstrates those words without actually using them in the text
    - Limit descriptions of a character to one killer sentence
    - Set up named opposing groups within

the world or town, each with their own appropriate symbol

- Why is today is different for the protagonist?
    - This is often the first clue leading up to the inciting incident—or it could even be the inciting incident.
- Is your protagonist self-protecting or self-sacrificing, and how can you show that?
    - The answer to this question will tell your reader whether your character is heroic or villainous.
    - Give the reader a reason to root for them / hate them based on the person they are, and not based on their background or situation. For example, Katniss gives up some of her food to one of the people at the Hob in the first chapter of *The Hunger Games*.
    - Have the reader save (or hurt) someone who is completely innocent (childlike) (a child, a small animal, a helpless stranger), as this makes a greater impact.
- What is the protagonist's fatal flaw?
    - Give your character's fatal flaw a symbol or story (tattoos, scars, nicknames, etc.) This allows you to keep reminding the

reader of the fatal flaw throughout the book

- The fatal flaw should be in direct conflict with the journey you're sending the character on
- Find a way to bring up your character's fatal flaw without making it so obvious to the reader

- What is the inciting incident or incidents?
  - This should be a surprising turn-of-fate type of moment
  - The inciting incident poses a question, and the protagonist will need to come up with an answer.
  - To make this more impactful, make the original plan and the protagonist's regular life very compelling to the character… it's HARD to leave it behind and the character is genuinely torn
- How does the character feel about the inciting incident?
  - What is the immediate emotional reaction to it?
  - If it makes sense, have the character enter a "5 Stages of Death" scenario with their

ordinary world and/or external goals

- Show the 5 stages of death without calling them out, through dialog, action, or narrative summary
- Get into the character's head and don't be afraid to spill their emotions over this conflict onto the page!

- What are the two decisions the protagonist faces?
  - The character grieved the two options in front of him or her and likes neither, but is resigned to their "fate."
  - They've acted out for a bit and then realize, "this is no way to live life." They move toward a decision.
  - How and when does the character accept their fate and the "new normal"?
  - Which decision sends them on the most exciting quest?

- What is the character's decision about the quest?
  - The decision is the answer to the question. That decision is the end of Part 1.
  - Give the character an actual scene where it hits them that these two choices are

their new reality (as they would have been resisting their journey up until then)

- Show the decision through action, not through narrative or in the mind of the character.

Press On, Igniter!

Day 27

OUTLINING 25-50%

Now, you are going to map out the rough beats for the middle 25-50% of the novel.

THE FAULT IN OUR STARS

Part 2: Hazel and Augustus face several obstacles here. Hazel has a health setback. They have trouble getting to Amsterdam. Once they get there, Peter van Houten, the author of *An Imperial Affliction*, refuses to give them a satisfying ending to the book. On the romance side, they have the conversation about how it would be a privilege to have his heart broken by her.

The Reversal: A few things happen in quick succession. They kiss at Anne Frank's house, then sleep together shortly after. This is a genre tentpole moment for romance. They are both all in on the relationship. The next day, though, Augustus admits that cancer is back, all over his body, and he only has a short time left to live.

ULTIMATE NOVEL PLOTTER: THE RESPONSE (25-50% OF YOUR NOVEL)

Use this template as a guide for completing the third section of the Ultimate Novel Plotter: The Response. I've included my questions plus some simple notes that may or may not help you refine your answers.

- How does the character process things right after The Decision is made?
  - There's often a regroup period while the shock of the decision (which your character is often thrust into) wears off. During this time, your character processes, prepares, and doubts himself and what he has gotten into. There's a lull before excitement starts.
  - The character may need to say goodbyes to people or places from old life.
  - The character may feel lost or be wondering, "okay, what now?"

- The character often meets mentors, sidekicks, and allies during this period. They may also meet some enemies for the first time.

- In some books, this point also includes a physical transition through transportation. For example, in both *Harry Potter* and *The Hunger Games*, the protagonist takes a train into their new reality.

- What happens to the character first on this new journey? What is his or her first move? Who is really in control?

  - List your false beliefs (stemming from the fatal flaw and motivation) in reverse order and start your character off with the easiest one to break through. What is his or her first goal? Does he or she have a choice, or must he go with the flow?

  - Keep in mind that the protagonist needs to start with easy challenges, that they may be fumbly or a little out of their comfort zone, and that they can succeed or fail at these initial breakthroughs.

  - Because the character is still in Wanderer Energy, it's likely that someone else is in control of their next move. For example, Harry Potter has to learn and conform to school rules and abide by his new class schedule. Katniss from *The Hunger Games* has to do what the gamemakers schedule for her, including getting a makeover, doing interviews in front of a live audience, and training in various survival and hunting skills.

- What is the antagonistic force sighting in this section?

  - Same as with false beliefs—list your "cronies" to the bad guy in reverse order and give your protagonist the easiest ones at the start of the book (boss at Level 1, Level 2).

  - The ideal antagonistic force sighting is some sort of henchman or reminder of the villain the hero will encounter at the end.

- What happens to the protagonist after the antagonistic force shows up?

  - Typically, the antagonistic force introduces more challenges.

  - Ideally, the challenges faced in this section encompass everything your character needs to do to break through false beliefs before they are ready to face the Reversal.

- What is The Reversal?
    - Something TOTALLY unexpected happens that threatens EVERYTHING the character knew and believed before. This is typically a critical piece of information that the protagonist doesn't have until now, even though sometimes, the reader can see it coming from a mile away. This is the internal arc of The Reversal.
    - The character looks death in the eye literally. In a thriller, there's no way out—the character thinks he's going to die. In an action/adventure, the character misses death by a hair or is rescued at the last minute. This is the external arc of The Reversal.
    - Decide what the internal arc and external arc would be for your protagonist and try to make The Reversal hit both. Ideally, the external is just a symbol for the internal. While you likely can get away with either the internal or external arc (depending on your genre), your book will be better if you hit both.
    - If you are writing something lighter like a romance or drama, it could be something like finding out the man you are falling in love with is still married (literal death

- of your relationship, which is a symbol of something else).

- The Reversal can even be a setback for them in changing their mindset.

- The protagonist should finally feel like things are calming down and they are getting the hang of things; the Reversal pulls out the rug from under them again.

- The thing or person that "dies" ideally ties directly back to the protagonist's fatal flaw. For example, in a romance novel, the Reversal would be the death of the relationship!

- The Reversal is like a dress rehearsal for the final battle. It should to some extent mirror or foreshadow what will happen at the end of the book.

Press On, Igniter!

Day 28
OUTLINING 50-75%

Next, you are going to map out the rough beats for the middle 50-75% of the novel.

THE FAULT IN OUR STARS

Part 3: They are both rocked by this huge setback in their relationship. Through this new lens of information, they set aside the goal to get the ending to An Imperial Affliction, for now. They spend a lot of time together actively trying to accept both of their deaths, when they finally decide they are going to write eulogies for each other. She writes his, but he is too sick to write hers.

The "Cards on the Table" Moment: At his fake funeral, she assures him that she is not angry at him for being the grenade that blew her up. She is so thankful for their "infinity." Shortly after, Augustus dies, and their time together has ended. All is lost.

ULTIMATE NOVEL PLOTTER: THE ATTACK (50-75% OF YOUR NOVEL)

Use this template as a guide for completing the fourth section of the Ultimate Novel Plotter: The Attack. I've included my questions plus some simple notes that may or may not help you refine your answers.

- How does The Reversal light up the protagonist? The other characters?
    - The protagonist is angry after The Reversal (usually) and motivated to take action. Show the transition between passively letting things happen vs. proactively attacking the problem.
    - During this charge up period, the protagonist starts to gather resources for a bigger battle. What new pieces of information, actual objects or weapons, new alliances, or new skills are needed?
- What are the big action steps the character takes? Who does he or she attack first?
    - The protagonist will have more false be-

lief(s) breakthroughs. The challenges are getting bigger and the fatal flaw is becoming more prominent.

- In this section, conquering an entire group here is stronger than a single person. For example, the protagonist could be a quarterback who wins a football game against a rival team. For Katniss in *The Hunger Games,* she attacks the career tributes' food supply, hoping to starve them all out.

- This is a good opportunity for the protagonist to get to the root of their emotional issues and break through a larger false belief that's been holding them back. It could also be an opportunity to re-trigger the fatal flaw.

- What is the antagonistic force sighting in this section?

  - This can be the actual villain or at perhaps right hand man. If it's the actual villain, both the villain and the hero must escape each other and live to fight another battle.

  - All of the villains thematically should believe in or have the same/similar values (Draco, Snape, Voldemort); they also have the same marks (Slytherin, the Death

Eater mark). Feel free to develop shades within the grouping.

- What other actions does the protagonist take? What else needs to happen going into the final battle?
  - The protagonist will have more false belief(s) breakthroughs. The challenges are getting bigger and the character is facing more and more tests—and succeeding more often.
  - The challenges are moving from somewhat dangerous (a Quidditch game) to very dangerous (life and death games). In an action/adventure/thriller/mystery, the character should be in a life or death situation. In a romance, the relationship should be barely surviving and on life support.
- What is the "Cards on the Table" Moment?
  - The character is often recouping and beginning to build resources just before this moment.
  - Then the last piece of information is revealed, and things move quickly. The character can no longer struggle with fear, confusion, worry, or anxiety. There are no excuses left. It's time. The charac-

ter is headed into the final battle no matter what.

Press On, Igniter!

Day 29
OUTLINING 75-100%

Finally, you are going to map out the rough beats for the last 75-100% of the novel.

THE FAULT IN OUR STARS

Part 4: Hazel tries to move through her grief, but these attempts mostly end in failure. She is very, very sad and there's no easy way to get past it. The enemy, death, has won. Peter van Houten tries to make amends with her, but she's not having it. She's just completely over her quest for the ending of *An Imperial Affliction*. But he does make her realize that it wasn't her goal to begin with; her real goal is to make sure her parents have lives after she is gone. She goes home and settles this with them, finally gaining peace of mind about her own death.

The Transformation: She receives Augustus's eulogy for her. In it, he asks her if she likes her choices about who got to hurt her in this world. She says, "I do," confirming that her fatal flaw, that she did not believe she should "leave her scar" on anyone, is completely overcome.

ULTIMATE NOVEL PLOTTER: THE RESOLUTION (75–100% OF YOUR NOVEL)

Use this template as a guide for completing the fifth section of the Ultimate Novel Plotter: The Resolution. I've included my questions plus some simple notes that may or may not help you refine your answers.

- What is your character's misguided goal going into the resolution?

    - The character starts the final battle with a goal. Because he or she doesn't quite know what lies ahead (and hopefully the reader doesn't either), this goal is always misguided. For example, Katniss originally just wanted to save herself and get back to District 12, but going into the final battle she now wants to save Peeta too. The goal is misguided because the Cap-

DAY 29 : OUTLINING

itol was never going to let two tributes win the games.

- The misguided goal is more aligned with who the character is now than who he or she was at the beginning of the book. Take into account all the false beliefs he or she has already broken through, and also consider the fatal flaw and the transformation the reader expects at the end of the book.

- The misguided goal is at the heart of the character's fatal flaw (but still misguided because the character hasn't fully broken through the fatal flaw yet). For Katniss, she's starting to feel hopeful about her future, potentially with Peeta. All of this will be washed away shortly as the book rolls toward its conclusion.

- What else needs to happen before the final battle can happen?

  - The final pieces fall into place to lead the protagonist into the ultimate battle, often through their own actions + external forces.

  - Leading up to the battle feels inevitable, like things rolling along at a quickening pace; you could incorporate a deadline here and thread that through earlier parts of the book too.

- For Harry, the ultimate battle in the first book is meeting Professor Quirrell, who has Voldemort growing out of the back of his head.

- What are the details of the battle?

  - Where does it take place? When?

  - What is the villain's fatal flaw? Use that to let the hero get the best of him in this fight. The villain's fatal flaw should be something that the hero doesn't have an issue with (it's the hero's strength)

  - What is the hero's clever moment? Usually this has been seeded earlier in the book. The hero has something the villain doesn't.

  - The battle is ideally not just between two people, but also between two ideologies/worldviews that are the foundation of the book's larger themes.

- How does the villain make a comeback after the hero's clever moment?

  - In every great climax, there is the Eye of the Storm. The hero thinks they've won. But... things are unsettling. There is something wrong.

- Draw out the tension and the "unsettling" part of this. Your audience will recognize it!

- Sometimes, this part (especially in movies) is where the villain tells the hero exactly how he did it. In *Harry Potter*, for example, Professor Quirrell explains how he defeated all of the challenges and tricked Harry over the course of the school year.

- In *The Hunger Games*, however, the comeback is eerier. Katniss and Peeta are waiting to be declared the winners, when the gamemakers come on overhead to tell them that only one can win.

- What is the villain's clever moment?

    - During the climax, there is One Last Battle With a Twist. The villain has a clever moment and corners the hero.

    - Have the villain strike the protagonist at the core of his fatal flaw. If the hero thinks everyone he loves is in more danger because of who he is, the villain has the love of his life in his clutches.

    - There's seemingly no way out for the hero... it takes every bit of the hero's energy to win. The hero has one last trick in his or her bag.

- In *The Hunger Games*, Katniss pulls out the poisoned berries and threatens to commit suicide with Peeta, leaving the gamemakers with no victor. In *Harry Potter*, Harry discovers that his mother's sacrifice has left Voldemort (merged with Professor Quirrell) unable to touch his skin.

- What are the last bits and pieces that must be wrapped up?

  - How do you want to reader to feel at the end of your book? Emotional? Crying? Insanely happy? (Hint: You should feel this way writing it!) Choose one word and make sure your ending hits the mark.

  - You must show that the character has experienced transformation and that he's not the same as he's always been. The fatal flaw is overcome! The villain represented or was tied to the fatal flaw in some way. For example, for Katniss, her hopelessness for the future is directly tied to the Capitol's rule over Panem.

  - Ideally, if the protagonist has gone on an adventure, he or she needs to return to where the adventure started. New hero

DAY 29 : OUTLINING

in an old environment demonstrates the contrast of their transformation visually.

- You must set up the next book or next action step(s). For example, *Twilight* does this by ending with a question of whether she'll be a vampire or not. It's an open ended question and allows for the book to become a series!

- If there are any lingering conversations to be had between characters to give the reader closure, now is the time to have them.

Press On, Igniter!

Day 30

FILL IN THE GAPS

You made it! Today is the last day of novel writing prep! Congrats!

Today is a day for celebration, so grab a glass of your favorite beverage (it need not be alcoholic, but if it is, why not?) and let's have a toast to making it to the last day of this book in one piece.

At this point, you have a huge document that goes deep into the ins and outs of your novel. Congratulations again on completing your Ultimate Novel Plotter document. That's huge!

Today, the task is simple. Go back through your notes. If there is anything more you want to add to your document, do so now.

Some people like to take the first section (The Treatment) and bring those notes into the other four sections, which are a bit more like an ordered outline. Specifically, they like to bring forward introductions

DAY 30: FILL IN THE GAPS

of characters, worldbuilding, and thematic elements to the four parts (The Setup, The Response, The Attack, and The Resolution). If there is anything you'd like to rearrange in your document, do so now.

If you are happy with your document, you need not do anything. You are cleared for writing your first draft. Go forth!

NEXT STEPS

Thank you so much for spending the past 30 days with me, jamming on your novel. I absolutely love working on story structure—it's one of my favorite things about being a writer—and I delighted in sharing what I know with you through this book.

I genuinely believe that these past 30 days have set you up for huge success on your first draft, and that your book is going to turn out great!

If there's anything you feel is missing from this book, please send your questions and suggestions to my team at team@theworldneedsyourbook.com. I'd love to help you out!

Additionally, if you want to go even deeper into story structure, you can learn my full Story Symmetry Framework in the book *Story Symmetry for Novelists: Tune Your Story Into Harmony and Alignment to Create a Better Reading Experience* (The Productive Nov-

elist #5).

It's available at all retailers!

WHAT NEXT?

For starters: write your first draft! You are ready!

Outside of writing your novel, you may be interested in working with me further. At The World Needs Your Book, I've created numerous resources that can help you draft, edit, publish, and market your book.

The Productive Novelist All-Access Pass

If you want to work with me through my self-study courses, you may be looking for an all-access pass! There are 8+ courses in this pass, ranging from storytelling to editing to writing faster to launching and marketing.

Through these products, we offer email support via team@theworldneedsyourbook.com + a general group where we answer questions.

To learn more, go to:

» **theworldneedsyourbook.com/shop**

The Productive Novelist Books

The Productive Novelist series is 14 books spanning all topics related to writing, editing, publishing, and marketing your book(s). There are also several advanced books in this series for those who intend to make writing a career and want to build their businesses for longevity. The content in this series has been tested by thousands of authors when it was originally published as the *Growth Hacking For Storytellers* series. We've since updated all the content and added several chapters to the newer editions.

To learn more and see what we have to offer, go to:

- » **theworldneedsyourbook.com/shop**

The Productive Novelist Channel, Podcast, and blog

I share tons of free content on my Youtube channel, podcast, and blog. Some people like to get right to the solution with a course or a book, while others like to receive a drip, drip, drip week-to-week through my Youtube channel or podcast feed. Please connect with me on my channels—I would love for you to subscribe!

- » **theworldneedsyourbook.com/blog**

YOUR FEEDBACK, PLEASE

My goal for writing this book is to help fiction authors write the best stories they possibly can and work on their craft.

There are two ways to leave feedback:

Reviews

If you loved this book, we can always use an honest review on our public retailer pages, where other people looking for the books can see what real people think of them.

Choose your retailer and leave a review here:

» **theworldneedsyourbook.com/reviewpn1**

Feedback Form

If you have anything you'd like to share privately, please feel free to fill out our feedback form here:

» **theworldneedsyourbook.com/feedback**

All answers are private unless you say we can use the responses publicly in our marketing materials.

HEARTFELT THANKS AND LOVE

Lastly, I want to say thank you so much for reading this book. I am fully aware that there are many, many people in the world who are trying to profit by stealing away your time and distracting you from your goals. As such, I hope your time with me has been entertaining, educational, and productive.

SPREAD THE WORD

Can you think of two people who could use this

book in their lives? Maybe a few other fiction writers who want to write their best story possible, or plan to participate in National Novel Writing Month (#NaNoWriMo)?

If so, I would love if you could connect them to this book so they too can prep an awesome novel and improve their craft easily and effectively.

Thanks again for reading.

Press on, Igniter!

ACKNOWLEDGEMENTS

Thank you to my readers who love jamming on story structure as much as I do. Let's keep being nerds together—it warms my heart and delights my soul!

A special thank you to my accountability group Kalvin Chinyere, Ember Casey, Alyssa Archer, Amy Teegan, Kerry McQuaide, and Claire Taylor. Your help is the only reason this book and series is in the world today!

ABOUT THE AUTHOR

Monica Leonelle was born in Germany and spent her childhood jet-setting around the world with her American parents. Her travels include most of the United States and Europe, as well as Guam, Japan, South Korea, Australia, and the Philippines.

She is a *USA Today* bestselling author best known for her young adult urban fantasy and paranormal romance series, *Waters Dark and Deep*, writing as Solo Storm. She also teaches writing, publishing, business, and marketing at **TheWorldNeedsYourBook.com**. Her three nonfiction series, *Growth Hacking For Storytellers*, *The Productive Novelist*, and *Book and Business Coaching*, have helped thousands of business owners and aspiring writers write faster, become better storytellers, and find their way to success.

Before becoming an independent author, Monica led digital marketing efforts at Inc. 100 companies like Hansen's Natural and Braintree.

Monica is a lifetime member of Sigma Pi Sigma honor fraternity and was a 2007 Chicago Business Fellow, graduating with an MBA from the Chicago Booth School of Business at 25 years old. She holds a Bachelor of Science in Computer Science with a minor in Physics from Truman State University.

She's been an avid blogger of marketing and business trends since 2007. Her ideas have been featured in *AdAge, Forbes, Inc.*, LinkedIn Voices, *The Huffington Post*, the AMEX OpenForum, *GigaOm, Mashable, Social Media Today*, and the *Christian Science Monitor*. In 2009, she was named one of the top 25 Tweeters in the city of Chicago by *ChicagoNow*, a subsidiary of the *Chicago Tribune*.

Visit **TheWorldNeedsYourBook.com** for email updates and additional resources.

Made in the USA
Las Vegas, NV
15 November 2022